THE BATTLE OF GETTYSBURG

A Guided Tour

Edward J. Stackpole
&
Wilbur Nye

Revised by Bradley M. Gottfried

STACKPOLE
BOOKS

0 11557 02676 4

Published by
STACKPOLE BOOKS
5067 Ritter Road
Mechanicsburg, PA 17055

Printed in the United States of America

10 9 8 7 6 5 4 3 2 1

Revised and Updated Edition

Cover illustration is a portion of Philipoteaux's cyclorama painting at Gettysburg National Military Park. Courtesy of the National Park Service
Cover Design by Caroline Stover
Composition by Lisa Palmer

Library of Congress Cataloging-in-Publication Data

Stackpole, Edward J. (Edward James), 1894-
    The Battle of Gettysburg : a guided tour / Edward J. Stackpole and Wilbur Nye — Rev. / by Bradley Gottfried.
      p.cm.
    Includes bibliographical references.
    ISBN 0-8117-2676-2
    1. Gettysburg National Military Park (Pa.)—Tours. 2. Gettysburg (Pa.), Battle of, 1863. I. Nye, Wilbur Sturtevant, 1898-1970. II. Gottfried, Bradley. III. Title.
E475.56.S73   1998
973.7'349—dc21
                                           98-2614
                                             CIP

HOW TO USE THIS TOUR GUIDE

This book has two parts: a tour guide and a short, thorough history of the battle. The sections are self contained; one can take the tour and get a good understanding of the battle without reading the history. The best approach, however, is to read the history before going on the tour. A third approach is to follow the tour and periodically flip back to the cross-listed history sections for a more thorough description of events at each stop.

For best results, before you leave each tour stop, read the directions to the next stop and what you should look for along the route. With few exceptions, the regular tour follows the National Park Service's three-hour tour route. General directions (such as "look to your left") are based on which way your car is facing. For clarity, Confederate leaders are italicized.

P A R T   I

THE TOUR GUIDE

A SHORT HISTORY
OF THE CAMPAIGN AND BATTLE

*G*eneral *Robert E. Lee* invaded Pennsylvania with his 70,000-man Army of Northern Virginia because he realized that no matter how many victories he won in Virginia, independence for the Confederacy would be gained only with a major victory on Northern soil. Stealthily moving his army northward, he outwitted his adversary, Major General Joseph Hooker, commander of the 95,000-man Army of the Potomac, and swept into Pennsylvania. One of *Lee's* divisions came within two miles of the state capital, Harrisburg, before being recalled. Hooker was replaced by Major General George Meade and the Northern army was quickly put into motion.

The forces collided at the town of Gettysburg on the morning of July 1, 1863. Here, Brigadier General John Buford's cavalry division held off two brigades of *Major General Henry Heth's* infantry division advancing from the west, until Major General John Reynolds' I Corps infantry arrived. Before noon on the first day, the battle favored the North. One Confederate brigade under *Brigadier General James Archer* was attacked as it crossed a stream; many of its men were captured by Brigadier General Solomon Meredith's famed Iron Brigade. A little later, a second brigade under *Brigadier General Joseph Davis* made the mistake of seeking refuge in a railroad cut. It proved to be a trap and, again, many Southerners fell into Union hands.

1

Around noon, a Confederate division under *Major General Robert Rodes*, part of *Lieutenant General Richard Ewell's* II Corps, descended upon the battlefield from the north and attacked Reynold's right flank. The attacks were badly coordinated, resulting in additional Southern repulses. Major General Oliver Howard's XI Corps arrived around 12:30 P.M. and took position north of town. Another of *Ewell's* divisions, under *Major General Jubal Early* hit Howard's right flank; after heavy fighting, the Federals retreated in confusion toward town. Meanwhile, *Heth's* division and a fresh one under *Major General Dorsey Pender* attacked the I Corps from the west, while *Rodes* attacked from the north. After intense fighting, they pushed the Federals back to Seminary Ridge and then to Cemetery Hill, south of town.

The first day ended without the Confederates sealing their victory by taking the hills south of Gettysburg. In the following two days, *Lee* tried to rectify this mistake by attacking the heights. The July 2 action did not begin until late afternoon, when two divisions under *Lieutenant General James Longstreet* attacked the southern part (left flank) of the Union line. Not satisfied with his position, Major General Daniel Sickles had moved his III Corps forward to occupy some high ground between Cemetery Ridge and Seminary Ridge. Soon after Sickles completed this ill-fated move, *Longstreet's* men viciously attacked at a number of sites, including Devil's Den/Rose's Woods, the Wheatfield, and the Peach Orchard. Intense fighting also occurred on Little Round Top, a fairly large hill that commanded the battlefield. During the early evening, a division under *Major General Richard Anderson* stormed Cemetery Ridge. One of his brigades pierced the Union line only to be pushed back with heavy losses. At the northern sector of the Union line, south of Gettysburg, Confederates attacked the two major hills, Cemetery and Culp's. Two of *Early's* brigades captured Cemetery Hill but were driven back in the darkness. One brigade of *Major General Edward Johnson's* division also took a portion of the Union trenches on Culp's Hill and remained there during the night. Except for the breach on Culp's Hill, the Confederates were unable to break the Union forces or capture and hold the high ground.

Day three (July 3) opened with a predawn clash between Major General Henry Slocum's XII Corps and *Johnson's* division. After fighting for seven hours on the heavily wooded slopes of Culp's Hill, the Confederates finally conceded. Then *Lee* made his most famous gamble—an attempt to break the center of the Union line on Cemetery Ridge with units from four divisions—about 13,000 men, including *Major General George Pickett's* fresh division of Virginians from *Longstreet's* corps. The magnificent charge failed, though the Confederates did breach the Union line. There were just too few men left at the end to do much damage.

Lee hoped that Meade would attack him and waited through July 4 for him to do so. When no assault came, he reluctantly withdrew into Virginia, ending the threat to the North.

BEGINNING THE TOUR

▶ Assuming that you are beginning your tour at the Gettysburg Visitor Center, set your trip odometer to zero, and leave the parking lot via the exit that faces the cemetery. Make a left onto Washington Street. Cross Baltimore Pike and turn left at the next traffic light (Middle Street), which is 0.8 mile from the visitor center. After the second traffic signal on Middle Street, look for Reynolds Avenue, which is the second street on the right, 1.9 miles from the visitor center.

☛ **ALONG THE WAY TO TOUR STOP 1.** As you drive through the town, try to visualize what it looked like in 1863. Many of the houses from the era of the battle remain and the streets are about the same width as they were then. If you look from side to side, you will see many side streets and alleys. This maze caused thousands of fleeing Union soldiers to lose their way and be captured by the Rebels on July 1. As you leave town, you ascend a steep ridge with a traffic light at its crest. This is Seminary Ridge. After heavy fighting on the morning of July 1, the Union I Corps took refuge here in the afternoon, but was driven back into the town. You can see Lutheran Theological Seminary on the right.

Reynolds Avenue runs along the top of still another elevation, McPherson's Ridge, where the first day's battle opened. On your right were the positions of Union troops who tried to stem the growing mass of Confederate troops, who were advancing in long, well-ordered lines from your left (west). The monuments and cannon show the units' positions during this phase of the battle. For example, the monument on your right, to the 121st Pennsylvania, with an interesting representation of a bursting artillery shell, shows its approximate position on the extreme left flank of the army. Attacked in the front and flank, it was forced to retire to Seminary Ridge to your right.

A few yards ahead, also on the right of the road, are two small stone markers. Ubiquitous on the battlefield, these flank markers show where one unit's line of battle ended and another's began. Each contains the name of the regiment and an "LF" (left flank) or an "RF" (right flank) designation. Because regiments formed next to one another to form long battle lines, these markers usually occur in pairs.

Farther along on your right is the monument to Major General Abner Doubleday, the Union commander in this sector during the first day's battle.

TOUR STOP 1. McPHERSON'S RIDGE. (SEE P. 49)

Stop just on the other side of Meredith Avenue (2.4 miles from the visitor center). During the morning of the first day's battle, this ridge was the site of heavy fighting between Reynolds' I Corps and *Heth's* division. The Iron Brigade arrived just as *Archer's* brigade moved through the woods to your left. McPherson's, or Herbst's woods, appear much as they did then, without, of course, clouds of smoke and ripping volleys of rifle fire. Reynolds was killed soon after he arrived on the scene. The spot is on your left, marked by a monument in front of the woods. To your right, in the background, is the seminary, including the cupola that the Union forces used as an observation platform during this phase of the battle.

➤   Continue along Reynolds Avenue to the traffic light and turn left onto Chambersburg Pike. Make another left turn at the first intersection, 0.15 mile from the light. This is Stone Avenue.

☛ **ALONG THE ROUTE TO TOUR STOP 2.** On the right side of Chambersburg Pike, just before it intersects with Stone Avenue, are statues of Generals Reynolds and Buford. The cannon astride the road mark the position of Calef's (and later Hall's) batteries, which caused hundreds of Southern casualties during the morning fight. One of the barrels on Buford's monument purportedly fired the first shell of the battle. On the left of Chambersburg Pike is a monument to one of the regiments of the Pennsylvania Bucktails that shows this unit's distinctive headgear. The soldier's gaze is toward a small but intrepid group of men who took the unit's flag to draw murderous fire away from the remainder of the regiment.

As you turn onto Stone Avenue, McPherson's white barn is on your left. Built during the mid-nineteenth century, it is all that remains of the original farm buildings. The barn was the center of severe fighting in the early afternoon, when Colonel Roy Stone's Pennsylvanians fought *Colonel John Brockenbrough's* Virginians attacking from your right and *Brigadier General Junius Daniel's* North Carolinians advancing from behind you. After gallantly holding off these attacks, the brigade was forced back to Seminary Ridge to your left.

Continuing, you see a statue of a man standing on a rock on the left side of the road. This commemorates a seventy-year-old Gettysburg resident, John Burns. Despite his age, this War of 1812 veteran ventured out to fight with the men of the Iron Brigade. Despite three wounds, he survived the battle. You are now at the right flank of the Iron Brigade, which held off *Heth's* attacks for several hours as the Confederates came down Herr Ridge to your right. First it threw back *Archer's* brigade about 9:30 A.M., then held off *Brockenbrough's* and *Brigadier General James Pettigrew's* brigades in the afternoon, until it was flanked and forced to retire to Seminary Ridge.

The markers and monuments on the right and left of the road show where the regiments of the Iron Brigade were positioned. The distances seem short, but a Civil War regiment numbered 400 to 700 men, standing shoulder to shoulder. This veteran brigade came storming onto the field in the morning, just as *Archer's* men approached the road from the right. *Archer* got half his brigade across Willoughby Run, where the road passes closest to the creek on the right. It was there that he was attacked by the Iron Brigade. The Confederates sustained many casualties; *Archer* and more than seventy of his men were captured.

As Stone Avenue bends to the left, it changes to Meredith Avenue and you see one of the few Confederate markers on the right side of the road. It commemorates the 26th North Carolina of *Pettigrew's* brigade. This unit lost more men than any other regiment in the battle—687 out of 840, or 82 percent—in the intense fighting here on July 1 as well as in storming Cemetery Ridge along with *Pickett's* division on July 3.

▶   At the stop sign, turn left to get back onto Reynolds Avenue, cross Chambersburg Pike, and continue until you reach a stop sign. Turn left onto Buford Avenue.

Soon after you cross Chambersburg Pike, you will drive over a slight rise in the road that goes over railroad tracks. At the time of the battle, excavation for the tracks was almost complete, but the rails had not yet been

The Rose Farm. These Confederate dead in a field adjacent to the Rose House were from Semmes's brigade. In their rapid advance to help their comrades capture the Wheatfield, they did not see Brooks's brigade take position in the woods in front of them. Sheets of bullets flew at the unsuspecting Confederates, leaving the field covered with their killed and wounded.

laid. While *Archer's* brigade was being routed by the Iron Brigade south of the Chambersburg Pike, a different situation was arising here. *Davis's* Mississippi brigade initially approached a Federal brigade under Brigadier General Lysander Cutler from in front of you and to your left. After driving back several of Cutler's regiments, *Davis* was suddenly attacked by the reserve regiment of the Iron Brigade (the 6th Wisconsin) and two of Cutler's regiments. Not knowing what to do, many of *Davis's* men jumped into the railroad cut for protection. The cut, however, proved a trap, as the sides were too steep for the men to get out. They were soon surrounded, and many were shot or forced to surrender.

The modern view of the Rose Farm is remarkably similar to 1863. Just off Emmitsburg Road, the farm is rarely visited by tourists. The current peacefulness of the setting belies the turmoil and destruction that occurred on July 2.

You might wish to park your car carefully by the side of the road just beyond the tracks. The soldier on the monument to the 14th Brooklyn (84th New York) on the left side of the road looks down on the trapped men in the railroad cut. Beyond this monument, you can see a small wooded area to the right of the tracks where many Confederate dead were buried. From 1872 to 1874, the Daughters of the Confederacy removed all the dead that could then be located and reinterred them in Southern cemeteries.

➤ Buford Avenue makes a sharp bend to the right. Proceed to the stop sign at Mummasburg Road and cross to Tour Stop 2 in front of you.

As you turn onto Buford Avenue, you get a good view of the fields on the left where *Davis's* men initially battled Cutler's brigade before the fiasco at the railroad cut. In the afternoon, *Daniel's* North Carolinians advanced across these fields to attack Stone's Pennsylvanians (behind you, along Chambersburg Pike).

Along this road you see monuments to Federal cavalry. Buford's division first held these lines against the Southern infantry before the Federal infantry arrived. Although outnumbered, the cavalrymen were equipped with Sharps' repeating rifles, which could be fired three times faster than traditional infantry rifles.

Just before the Mummasburg Road, you see a knoll with a monument to the 17th Pennsylvania Cavalry on the right. This is the approximate location of the Forney farmhouse. The Confederates used it as a hospital and performed many operations there. In those days, when a soldier was hit in the arm or leg with a large-caliber bullet, the bones were often shattered beyond repair, and about the only treatment was amputation. Although many surgeons quickly became skillful, little was known about proper sanitation, and infection was a common result. During the first three days of July 1863, the Forney house was filled with gore. Scores of severed limbs were carried across the road (toward the Peace Light Monument in front of you) and buried in two rectangular trenches near where there is now a lone tree. The slight depression marking these trenches is visible in the stubble field beside the Mummasburg Road. You can best see this tree from the next tour stop.

TOUR STOP 2. ETERNAL PEACE LIGHT MEMORIAL.
(SEE P. 56)

This memorial was dedicated by President Franklin D. Roosevelt on July 3, 1938, on the seventy-fifth anniversary of the battle. Walk up to the monument and face south (the direction you came from), orienting on McPherson's white barn directly in front of you in the distance across the Chambersburg Pike.

When *Major General Robert Rodes* arrived here on Oak Hill around noon on July 1, he deployed his division in battle formation and positioned his artillery on this high ground. The batteries engaged the Federal artillery for an hour, then *Rodes* attacked with three brigades. Their mission was to destroy the Union right flank, which was anchored in the woods in front of you and to the left, on the other side of the Mummasburg Road. *Colonel Edward O'Neal's* brigade attacked on the far (east) side of the woods to your left, *Brigadier General Alfred Iverson's* brigade moved south across the open field in front of you and angled toward the woods (and the Federal flank), and *Daniel's* brigade advanced to your right, moving in the direction from which you just came. The attack was supposed to be coordinated but it came piecemeal, and two of the three brigades were smashed, as you will see at the next tour stop.

On the left of the monument (as you face it) are two English-made Whitworth guns. The Confederates had four of these breech-loading pieces, which could fire a shell five miles.

➤   Continue along the road you were on, cross the Mummasburg Road, and park at the tower on your left.

☛ **ALONG THE WAY TO TOUR STOP 3.** As the road from the peace memorial winds to the right and then straightens, you follow some of the ground covered by *O'Neal's* brigade as it attacked the Union right flank in front of you, on the other side of the Mummasburg Road.

As you cross the road, you see the unusual monument to the 90th Pennsylvania on your left. It is shaped like a tree and features military equipment and a robin's nest. As this area was torn by artillery fire, an occupied robin's nest was found in a shattered tree. Risking harm, a soldier grabbed the nest, climbed the remaining part of the tree, and placed it back on a branch. Part of Baxter's brigade, this regiment held the extreme right of the Federal line.

TOUR STOP 3. OAK RIDGE OBSERVATION TOWER.
(SEE P. 56)

Examine the historical map, then ascend the tower. Face the line of trees along the road where there is a low stone wall. Brigadier General Henry Baxter's Federal brigade was behind this wall facing *O'Neal's* North Carolinians, who were advancing along the foot of the slope, about where the railroad is now. After repulsing this charge, the Federals jumped over the wall and faced the open field beyond the trees along the side of the road. Advancing as if on parade, *Iverson's* brigade was met by a hail of bullets. So sudden and severe was the fire that the men fell in orderly ranks. The brigade lost 65 percent of its strength within a matter of minutes. Some 500 were later buried in the field about 200 yards in front of you. After these bodies were exhumed and taken south after the war, there remained circular depressions in this field called "*Iverson's* pits," but these are no longer noticeable. For years after the battle, the area around the pits could be discerned by a more luxuriant growth of crops. Ghost stories abounded in this part of the battlefield and many refused to work the fields after dark. Baxter's men also captured hundreds of Confederates.

Confederate strength was mounting, however, and the Union troops were forced from this position. While most of the Federals made for the rear, the 16th Maine acted as a rear guard. The small stone markers on either side of Doubleday Avenue, next to Mummasburg Road, mark this gallant regiment's position. It lost more than 80 percent of its men while defending its comrades' flight toward safety. Just before the regiment's flag was captured, the men ripped it to pieces, rather than allow it to fall into enemy hands.

Now move to the opposite side of the tower. Up to this point, the battle was being waged only by one of Meade's seven corps, Reynolds' I Corps. About 12:30 P.M., Major General Oliver Howard's XI Corps marched north through Gettysburg and formed a defensive line along the road, which is marked by cannon and monuments. Howard's men were soon hit on their right flank by a fresh Confederate division under *Major General Jubal Early* and driven back through the town.

You may want to visit the site of the fighting between the XI Corps and *Early's* division, which is part of Optional Tour A at the end of the Tour Guide section. This trip will take fifteen to twenty minutes.

➤ Reset your trip odometer and continue on Doubleday Avenue, following the arrow to the two-hour tour. The road makes several sharp right turns before coming to a stop sign. Turn left at the stop sign (Reynolds Avenue).

☛ **ALONG THE WAY TO TOUR STOP 4.** As you drive away from the tower, you get a good view of Forney's Field on your right, over which *Iverson's* men made their ill-fated charge. The marker in the center of the field shows where the 88th Pennsylvania counterattacked, capturing two battle flags and many prisoners. Also on this side of the road is the monument to the 11th Pennsylvania, which features a soldier at the ready. At its base, facing the open field, is carved a small dog that represents the regiment's mascot. Separated from the brigade after the first day's battle, "Sallie" stood vigil over the regiment's dead and dying here during the rest of the conflict. The dog was killed two years later while going into battle with her many masters. The men so loved their little pet that they insisted she be immortalized with them on the monument.

As you approach Chambersburg Road, you see the monument to the 143d Pennsylvania across the road under two pine trees, which commemorates the unit's color guard. Forced to retreat in the afternoon toward Seminary Ridge, the color guard stopped several times to defiantly wave his flag and shake his fist at the Confederates. Both sides mourned this brave soldier when he was killed during the retreat.

> Turn left onto the Chambersburg Road and drive 0.2 mile (or 1.1 miles from the Oak Hill tower) to the first road on your right, Seminary (or Confederate) Avenue (which may not be marked). Turn right here and proceed across the intersection with Hagerstown Pike (Middle Avenue). Seminary Avenue is now called West Confederate Avenue.

☛ **ALONG THE WAY TO TOUR STOP 4.** While still on Chambersburg Pike, just before you reach West Confederate Avenue, you see *Lee's* headquarters on your left. As you turn onto Seminary Avenue, you pass the stone wall on your left that was constructed by *Rodes's* division. You are now on Seminary Ridge, the major Confederate position on the second and third days of the battle. During the late afternoon of July 1, remnants of the I Corps made their last stand here after being pushed off McPherson's Ridge to your right. Standing wheel to wheel, eighteen Union cannon shelled the onrushing Confederates. In front of the ridge to your right, *Brigadier General Alfred Scales's* brigade (*Pender's* division) took heavy losses. On the other side of the building with the cupola, *Colonel Abner Perrin's* brigade finally breached the Union line, forcing it back to Gettysburg.

After you cross Hagerstown Pike and pass several houses on your left, you see Cemetery Ridge on your left, about three-quarters of a mile away. This was the major Union position during the second and third days of the battle and the target of many Confederate attacks. On the right of the road, you see tablets representing the second- or third-day positions of various Confederate brigades. You also see a variety of cannon on both sides of the road. The armies used three main types:

1. 12-pounders (Napoleons). The bronze barrels are usually green and the breech has a knob. These were the most common cannon used in the battle, comprising around 40 percent of the artillery. Because

Gettysburg Looking East from Seminary Ridge. Some of the victorious Confederates saw this view as they advanced into the town during the afternoon of July 1.

The modern view, looking toward Gettysburg. The town has expanded greatly since 1863. You can see this view from the vicinity of Lee's Headquarters, between Tour Stops 2 and 3.

their barrels were not rifled, their range was short (less than a mile) but they were very effective against infantry.

2. Parrott rifles. These cannon, distinguished by their reinforced breeches, could fire a shell more than three miles.

3. Three-inch ordinance rifles. The small, smooth barrels with a knobbed breech were lightweight pieces with a range of more than two miles.

Each cannon could fire four different types of ammunition:

1. Solid shot. This projectile, much like a bowling ball, was fired into infantry at long range, knocking over soldiers and creating large gaps in formations.

2. Shells. These were filled with black powder that was ignited with a fuse. The projectiles exploded within enemy formations.

3. Case. Filled with about seventy-five small iron balls and black powder, this projectile showered metal among infantry when it exploded.

4. Canister. This was a metal can, containing about twenty-five one-inch balls that ruptured upon firing. The effect was similar to that of a shotgun, devastating to close infantry.

TOUR STOP 4. NORTH CAROLINA AND TENNESSEE STATE MEMORIALS.

The battlefield features a remarkable number of monuments to Union units and commanders but few commemorating the Confederates. The disparity had a variety of reasons, including a reluctance by Union authorities to allow such monuments on the field during the late nineteenth century, the lack of resources (each unit or state paid for their own markers; the U.S. government paid for the descriptive location tablets), and the South's unwillingness to commemorate perhaps its worst defeat.

The situation changed in the early twentieth century, when the Southern states began erecting monuments. As you drive along this road, you see all of the state memorials. North Carolina's was one of the earliest ones. Created in 1929 by Gutzon Borglum, the artist who carved Mount Rushmore, it commemorates the Confederate state that sent more men to this battlefield than any other except Virginia.

On July 3, the third day of the battle, *Brigadier General James J. Pettigrew's* North Carolina brigade assembled here before its advance against the Union forces behind you on Cemetery Ridge. This has become known as

Pickett's Charge but the attack actually was made by parts of three divisions. The monument attempts to tell what was occurring that day. The wounded man points out the location of the enemy to two young soldiers, who stands before an older veteran whispering words of encouragement. Borglum used photographs of Southern soldiers as his models, including the flag bearer, Orren Randolph Smith, who designed the Confederate "Stars and Bars" flag.

A short walk beside the stone wall along the road brings you to the Tennessee monument. The three figures represent the three Volunteer State regiments present at Gettysburg. The base of the monument is sixteen feet long; Tennessee was the sixteenth state to enter the Union. Part of the base is cut out to represent the shape of the state. Part of *Archer's* brigade, these regiments fought farther north, along McPherson's Ridge on July 1. The monument was erected here, their jumping-off spot during *Pickett's* charge.

☛ **ALONG THE WAY TO TOUR STOP 5.** As you drive toward Tour Stop 5, you see markers for the brigades in *Heth's* (commanded by *Pettigrew*) and *Pender's* divisions. These units joined *Pickett's* men on their desperate charge on the center of the Union line during the afternoon of July 3.

TOUR STOP 5. VIRGINIA MEMORIAL. (SEE P. 98)

This monument honors both *Robert E. Lee* and the Virginians who served under him at Gettysburg. The seven figures at the base represent men who joined the ranks from all walks of life. It is from this site that *Lee* observed *Pickett's* Charge. If you look closely at Cemetery Ridge behind you, you will see the clump of trees that was *Pickett's* target. After two days of battle, it came down to a frontal assault by *Pickett's* division and two others lined up north of you.

Walk along the path next to the woods, which takes you closer to Cemetery Ridge, where you can better see the ground that *Pickett's* men covered and some of the features of the ridge.

☛ **ALONG THE WAY TO TOUR STOP 6.** You pass the Florida memorial on your right. The three stars on the lighter-colored tablet represent the three small Florida regiments on the battlefield. They were part of *Perry's* brigade and saw action on the second and third days.

On your right is a sign for the monument to Berdan's Sharpshooters in Pitzer's Woods. During the afternoon of July 2, Major General Daniel Sickles, commander of the Union III Corps on Cemetery Ridge, was worried that

Confederates were massing for an attack. To find out, he sent Berdan's Sharpshooters and the 3d Maine to reconnoiter these woods. These troops came face to face with *Brigadier General Cadmus Wilcox's* brigade of *Major General Richard Anderson's* division. A sharp twenty-five minute fight ensued. The small Union force retreated back to Cemetery Ridge and informed Sickles that his worst fears were about to be realized.

TOUR STOP 6. PITZER WOODS. LOUISIANA AND MISSISSIPPI MEMORIALS. (SEE P. 84)

(SEE P. 84)

The reclining figure on the Louisiana memorial is that of a fallen artilleryman who is clutching a Confederate battle flag to his heart. Above him is a figure meant to represent either the "Spirit of the Confederacy" or St. Barbara, the patron of artillerymen. In one hand, she holds a flaming cannonball and below her, in the reeds, is a dove of peace.

A bit farther on is the Mississippi memorial. It was from this vicinity that *Brigadier General William Barksdale's* Mississippi brigade of *Major General Lafayette McLaws's* division attacked on July 2. The monument shows a Mississippi soldier defending a fallen flag bearer.

Both memorials feature a prostrate figure and toes protruding through tattered shoes.

ALONG THE WAY TO TOUR STOP 7. After crossing Millerstown Road, you see an observation tower to your left that offers panoramic views of the second day's battle and the Eisenhower Farm.

The unit tablets you have been passing belong to *McLaws's* division, which fell upon the Union positions at the southern end of Cemetery Ridge, the Peach Orchard, and the Wheatfield on July 2, finally driving back the Northern troops after exceptionally heavy fighting. You will visit these sites shortly.

After passing the Georgia monument and the South Carolina memorial (which contains an excerpt from the song "Ode at Magnolia Cemetery," sung when decorating Confederate graves in 1867) on the right, you come to the Arkansas memorial. Though only one of its regiments participated in the battle, the state erected this monument soon after the battle's centennial. The four small squares at each end of the monument with Confederate battle flags imprinted on them are made of aluminum, an abundant Arkansas resource.

After you cross Emmitsburg Road, you see the modest Texas memorial on the right, which belies the amount of fighting done by the three Lone Star regiments on July 2. Directly to your left, you see both Little Round Top and Round Top in the distance. Unoccupied when the Confederates attacked, they saw vicious fighting during the late afternoon and early evening of the second day.

The last Southern state monument honors Alabamans. Positioned approximately where *Brigadier General Evander Law's* Alabama brigade launched its attack on Little Round Top and Devil's Den, it represents the "Spirit of Alabama" in the center, which is comforting a wounded soldier on the left while encouraging the soldier on the right. The cartridge belt is being symbolically passed between the soldiers.

TOUR STOP 7. WARFIELD RIDGE. (SEE P.76)

Warfield Ridge is a continuation of Seminary Ridge and was important during the battle as the jumping-off spot for a powerful division commanded by *Major General John Bell Hood.*

On the right side of the road is the Soldiers and Sailors of the Confederacy Memorial. Erected at the end of the centennial, it honors all states that contributed personnel to the Confederate cause. On the base is the name Walter Washington Williams, the last surviving Confederate soldier, who died on December 19, 1959, at the age of 117.

ALONG THE WAY TO TOUR STOP 8. As you leave Tour Stop 7, you pass a stone fence that was built for protection during the evening of July 2, after some of *Hood's* troops had been forced back from the Wheatfield.

Entering a wooded area, you see a handsome monument to William Wells on your right. A commander of the 1st Vermont Cavalry, he participated in Brigadier General Elon Farnsworth's foolhardy charge against infantry during the late afternoon of the last day of the battle. Cavalry rarely does well against infantry, and this charge was no exception.

Signs for the Round Top trail indicate that you have reached this large hill. Because of its steepness and heavy woods, it was of much less tactical value than its sister, Little Round Top. Along the trail are monuments to units of the V and VI Corps that occupied the hill on the evening of July 2, after forcing two Alabama regiments of *Law's* brigade to vacate this high ground.

After you pass the intersection with Warren Avenue, you see the monument to the 83d Pennsylvania on the left side of the road. At its top is a statue of Colonel Strong Vincent, the 83d's brigade commander. The brigade valiantly defended Little Round Top on July 2. When Pennsylvania gave money to regiments for monuments, there was a restriction against memorials to individual soldiers. The 83d got around this by placing an unmarked figure atop the monument that all knew was Vincent.

Opposite this monument, on the right side of the road, you see the remains of a stone wall built by Vincent's men during the battle.

TOUR STOP 8. LITTLE ROUND TOP. (SEE P.77)

Park in the spaces along the left side of the road and walk along one of the trails in front of you. These lead to the summit of Little Round Top and show why this hill was so important to both armies. Artillery placed here commanded large areas of the battlefield and the hill formed the extreme left flank of the Union army. Sickles's III Corps was ordered to hold this hill and the part of Cemetery Ridge to your right. Fearing that the Confederates would take Houck's Ridge, the high ground in front of you nearer Emmitsburg Road, he moved his entire command forward to a vulnerable position during the afternoon of July 2. Soon after, he was assailed by three Confederate divisions and driven back after heavy fighting at Devil's Den, Rose's Woods, the Wheatfield, and the Peach Orchard.

On July 2-3, the Union line resembled a fishhook. You are standing on the extreme left flank of it. If you look directly to your right, you see the shank of the hook, which continued past the domed memorial to Pennsylvania troops, looped around Cemetery Hill, and ended on Culp's Hill, the barb of the hook.

Walk to your right to the statue of Brigadier General Gouverneur Warren. Face west (the direction you were traveling when you walked up the path) and you can see nearly the entire July 2 battlefield. On your left is Round Top, at the foot of which, across Plum Run, is Devil's Den, where gigantic boulders can be seen. Confederate sharpshooters held the boulders during the early evening of July 2, picking off Federal soldiers on this hill. On the distant ridge beyond Devil's Den, where you see cars moving along the highway, is Tour Stop 7 (Warfield Ridge), which we already saw was where *Hood's* attack began. To the right of Devil's Den, almost directly in front of you but obscured by the trees, is the Wheatfield, the site of tremendous charge and countercharge as neither side would willingly give up the field. Farther to the right, a white barn beyond the woods marks the Trostle farm, which played an important role after Union troops were driven out of the Peach Orchard (obscured by the trees).

One of the many heroes of the battle, Warren realized that the hill was unoccupied and rushed troops there just as the Confederates were about to capture it. A number of markers aid in understanding what happened here. Warren's dire warning brought Vincent's brigade to the hill. Confederate infantry made multiple attacks to your left and came close to capturing the hill.

Devil's Den. After the Confederates captured this field of large boulders, sharpshooters moved in and killed and wounded a number of Union troops on Little Round Top. This photograph shows one of the sharpshooters who met his fate on July 2.

Modern view of Devil's Den. The rock formation is little changed since 1863. This area can be seen on your right soon after you leave Tour Stop 8A.

Walk to your left toward the "castle." You will pass the memorial to the 140th New York, which bolstered Vincent's right flank just as it was being driven back. Prominently displayed on the memorial is a representation of Colonel Patrick O'Rorke, commander of the 140th, who was killed leading the successful counterattack. The monument is on the spot where he was killed. A number of other Union officers were killed here, including Vincent; another brigade commander, General Stephen Weed; and the commander of Hazelett's battery.

What looks like a castle in front of you is really the 44th and 12th New York monument. The tower is forty-four feet high and the main room measures twelve feet square. To the left of the 44th New York stood the 83d Pennsylvania, whose monument and position were seen on the approach to Little Round Top. To the left of the 83d Pennsylvania was the 20th Maine, immortalized in books and movies. It held the extreme left of the Union position and beat off attack after attack by two Alabama regiments. To reach the 20th's position and monument, which faces Round Top, return to the road and follow the marked path on the other side of it. The very ordinary monument there marks the center of Colonel Joshua Chamber-lain's line, where the U.S. flag was perched to inspire the men. You can also see the remains of the stone wall defended by the men of the 20th Maine.

➤ This tour will now take a side trip to Devil's Den and the Slaughter Pen, so you will be diverted for a short distance from the park service's auto tour. Get back into your car, reset your trip odometer, and continue driving for about 0.2 mile until you come to a stop sign. Turn left onto Wheatfield Road and proceed 0.4 mile from Little Round Top to Crawford Avenue. Turn left and proceed to Devil's Den.

☞ **ALONG THE WAY TO TOUR STOP 8A.** As you drive along Crawford Avenue, you cross Plum Run. This area was called the Valley of Death because of the intense fighting during the evening of July 2, which left the ground littered with almost 900 dead and wounded from both sides. Crawford's Pennsylvania Reserve division charged from the vicinity of Little Round Top into the victorious Confederates moving into this area from your right. After heavy fighting, Crawford stopped their advance. A statue of him is on the left of the road.

➤ Park in the spaces on the left side of the road. As you pull into a parking spot, the Slaughter Pen will be in front of you and Devil's Den behind you.

TOUR STOP 8A. DEVIL'S DEN. (SEE P. 80)

Two regiments of *Law's* brigade smashed into Ward's brigade (Birney's division, III Corps) in these two areas. After Devil's Den was claimed by the Confederates, sharpshooters moved in to pick off Union troops on Little Round Top. The fighting was particularly intense in the Slaughter Pen, where more than 200 dead and wounded Confederates were found after the battle. You may walk along the trails that wind through the curious granite boulders of Devil's Den.

➤ Continue on Crawford Avenue, which becomes Ayres Avenue, back onto the park service's auto tour route.

☞ ALONG THE WAY TO TOUR STOP 9. Just past Devil's Den are some cannon and a statue of a cannoneer on the right side of the road. They indicate the position of Smith's battery. The object of several Confederate attacks, this battery kept the Rebels at bay, causing hundreds of casualties, particularly in a small triangular field to the left of the road surrounded by stone fences. A bit farther along to the right is the monument to the 124th New York. Part of Ward's brigade, this regiment first battled regiments from *Brigadier General Jerome Robertson's* brigade and then *Brigadier General Henry Benning's* brigade. Its monument shows its commander standing with crossed arms as he tried to calm his men. He was later killed. In the end, the Union troops here were overwhelmed and three of Smith's cannon were captured. During the battle, this road did not exist and the ridge was not so heavily wooded.

TOUR STOP 9. WHEATFIELD. (SEE P. 82)

The Wheatfield was much more extensive in 1863 than it is now. Into this field surged thousands of men from parts of ten Union and four Confederate brigades. The Confederates attacked from your left and the Union troops arrived from your right. Fed in piecemeal, units from both sides took turns driving one another out of the field, until the Confederates finally gained control. Driving on, the Confederate brigades were hit by Crawford's division in the Valley of Death and thrown back beyond the Wheatfield.

➤ Continue along Ayres Avenue. At the dead end, turn left onto Wheatfield Road. Turn right onto Sickles Avenue, the first road on your right (2.0 miles from Little Round Top). Tour Stop 10 is found just as you turn into Sickles Avenue.

☛ **ALONG THE WAY TO TOUR STOP 10.** The monument on your left with the large cross is a tribute to the Irish Brigade. Although this famous unit contained three New York regiments and one each from Massachusetts and Pennsylvania, only the New Yorkers are represented because their state paid for the monument. At the base is an Irish wolfhound representing faith and devotion. Monuments to the other two regiments of the brigade are farther along this road.

Behind the 5th Michigan monument on your right are boulders with a bronze plaque marking the site of a forward field hospital of the 32d Massachusetts. Only fifty yards behind the front line, this makeshift facility provided emergency aid.

As the road makes a sharp loop to the right, you see a monument on the left with a soldier with his back to the road, holding what looks to be a broken gun. This monument to the Andrews Sharpshooters was not vandalized—it was merely a miscalculation by the artist, who ran out of granite.

The 116th Pennsylvania's monument on the left of the road at the "Loop" shows a fallen member of the Irish Brigade surrounded by broken accouterments.

Soon after you turn onto Wheatfield Road, you see cannon and a monument to the 9th Massachusetts (Bigelow's) Battery on the right. Never in battle before, this battery created havoc in the Confederate ranks that were advancing in front of you to the Peach Orchard and, to your left, at troops advancing through the Rose farm to the Wheatfield. After the Confederates took these areas, the battery was almost surrounded, so the gunners pulled the guns back to the Trostle farm, marked by the white house across the pasture, behind the monument. Using long ropes to save the horses, the men continued firing these guns while pulling them to safety. They continued to fire from the farm until they were overrun, losing nearly a third of their men and 80 percent of their horses, but Bigelow still saved a portion of his battery. More than three tons of ammunition was fired by this battery during this engagement. At the end of Trostle's barn you may be able to see a hole in the brick work below the two "diamonds," which was made by a Confederate shell. You will drive past the farmhouse soon.

TOUR STOP 10. PEACH ORCHARD. (SEE P. 84)

The Peach Orchard behind you and the area along Emmitsburg Road just to your left formed the right flank of Major General David Birney's division (Sickles's III Corps). Birney's three brigades occupied Devil's Den/Rose's Woods on its left flank, the Wheatfield in the center, and the Peach Orchard on the right. Each was separately overrun by *McLaws'* and *Hood's* divisions in the late afternoon and early evening of July 2. Like the Wheatfield, the Peach Orchard was more extensive in 1863. Advancing in perfect order from Seminary Ridge, *Barksdale's* Mississippi brigade attacked Brigadier General Charles Graham's brigade along Emmitsburg Road. Graham's men were driven back but regrouped in the Peach Orchard behind you. They again attempted to hold the Confederates but were driven out with heavy losses. The Confederates bagged almost 1000 prisoners here, including Graham. The Confederates then turned their attention to Cemetery Ridge, the heart of the Union position, which is in front of you and to your right.

The conical monument to the right of the road marks the spot where the commander of the 7th New Jersey was killed during the defense of the Peach Orchard.

> Continue along Sickles Avenue until you come to a dead end. Turn right onto United States Avenue (2.2 miles from Little Round Top). Cross Plum Run again and Tour Stop 11 is on your right.

ALONG THE WAY TO TOUR STOP 11. As you drive along Sickles Road, you parallel the position of Graham's troops along Emmitsburg Road before they were driven back by *Barksdale's* brigade to your left. As you drive along United States Avenue, you pass the Trostle farmhouse on your left, the scene of Bigelow's heroic stand against *Barksdale*. He was able to hold back the Confederates until additional artillery could be placed near Plum Run.

TOUR STOP 11. PLUM RUN. (SEE P. 85)

(SEE P. 85)

Although not marked with many memorials, the ground to the left of the road, behind Plum Run, was important in the repulse of *Barksdale's* Mississippians, who had crushed the Union position at the Peach Orchard. A number of cannon were hastily assembled here and held up the advance. Charging from your left, Willard's New York brigade threw the Mississippians back before they could reach Cemetery Ridge.

> Continue along United States Avenue until you reach a dead end. Make a right onto Hancock Avenue (2.9 miles from Little Round Top). Bear left at the fork and park at Tour Stop 12.

☞ **ALONG THE WAY TO TOUR STOP 12.** After turning onto Hancock Avenue, you are on Cemetery Ridge. This was the area that Sickles's second division under Major General Andrew Humphreys was supposed to hold. Instead, Sickles moved it forward to an exposed position along Emmitsburg Road to your left. The division was attacked by two brigades of *Anderson's* division along its front and *Barksdale's* brigade on its flank, and was driven back to Cemetery Ridge.

On the right of the road is the monument to Father William Corby, chaplain of one of the Irish Brigade regiments. The brigade occupied this area before its move to the Wheatfield, where it halted the Confederate advance before it was cut to pieces by a vicious flank attack. Before leaving the area, Father Corby mounted this large rock and granted the men absolution so long as they did their duty in battle. Father Corby later became president of the University of Notre Dame. A copy of this statue is on that campus.

TOUR STOP 12. PENNSYLVANIA MEMORIAL/ 1ST MINNESOTA MEMORIAL. (SEE P. 86)

On the right side of the road is the Pennsylvania Memorial, the largest monument on the battlefield. Erected in 1910 at a cost of $182,000, it is topped with a twenty-one-foot-high statue, the Goddess of Victory and Peace, made with bronze from cannonbarrels used in the war. Each side honors a branch of the service, and the eight statues recognize the most important Pennsylvanians on the battlefield that day. Tablets along the base are inscribed with the names of the 34,500 Pennsylvanians who were at Gettysburg.

The tall monument with a soldier running with a bayonet on the left of the road honors the heroic actions of the 1st Minnesota regiment on July 2. As *Wilcox's* brigade of *Anderson's* division threw back Humphreys' division and approached Cemetery Ridge, it was counterattacked by this small unit and driven back. The 1st Minnesota lost more than 80 percent of its men in a fight that lasted only minutes. The unit was never the same after the battle, but it had plugged a critical hole in the Union line. This was one of the most dramatic episodes of the entire battle and demonstrated how a relatively few men can influence the outcome. This heroic regiment lost seventeen of its survivors in helping repel *Pickett's* Charge the next day. The location of the monument corresponds to the starting point of the counterattack on July 2.

> Continue a short distance until you come to a road on your right. Turn onto it (Pleasonton Avenue), following the arrow to the three-hour tour, and continue until the road dead-ends at Taneytown Road (3.6 miles from Little Round Top). Turn left and drive 0.4 mile (4.2 miles from Little Round Top) and make a right onto Hunt Avenue. This road dead-ends at Baltimore Pike (4.7 miles from Little Round Top). Make a right onto Baltimore Pike. After about 0.3 mile (5.1 miles from Little Round Top), you will see a sign for the auto tour. Make a left here and, at the stop sign, turn right. At the next stop sign, drive ahead to Tour Stop 13 and park.

ALONG THE WAY TO TOUR STOP 13. You are driving in the rear of the Union line. It was loaded with reserve infantry, ammunition, wagons, and other resources needed to support an army in battle. Before reaching Taneytown Road, you pass the Hummelbaugh house on your left, one of the more than 100 hospitals established during the battle to care for the 30,000 wounded. Across from Hunt Avenue is the Lydia Leister house, site of Meade's headquarters for most of the battle. After you pass the second stop sign after leaving Baltimore Pike, note the two monuments on either side of the road. We will discuss them shortly.

TOUR STOP 13. SPANGLER'S SPRING. (SEE P. 97)

You are at the base of Culp's Hill, the right flank of the Federal army and the site of heavy fighting during the evening of July 2 and morning of July 3. During the early evening of July 2, Meade pulled all but Brigadier General George Greene's brigade of the XII Corps out of their entrenchments north of here on Culp's Hill to aid Sickles at the opposite end of the line. Meade did not know that *Lee* had ordered this hill to be captured at the same time that *Longstreet's* divisions were attacking the Federal left flank. *Johnson's* division moved against the entrenchments at night and, after several attacks, *Brigadier General George Stuart's* brigade finally captured some of them. We will see this area between Tour Stops 13 and 14. Early the next morning, parts of three Confederate divisions again tried to drive the Federals off this vital hill. The XII Corps, during the night, had reoccupied its original positions. For seven hours, waves of Confederates assailed the lines. All of these attacks failed and finally the Confederates pulled back, leaving large number of casualties.

Walk to the Indiana memorial in Spangler's Meadow to your right. Face the memorial and look to your right, where you will see the two memorials pointed out earlier. The monuments are to two regiments of Brigadier General Thomas Colgrove's brigade (Brigadier General John Geary's division, XII Corps), which advanced across this field on the morning of July 3. Charging from right to left, they were met by a killing fire from two Confederate brigades behind the stone wall to your left. The marker in the center of the field shows the farthest advance of the 27th Indiana before it was forced back to safety. The 2d Massachusetts continued but also was forced to retreat after taking heavy losses.

Turn around and walk to the springs behind you. While Colgrove's regiments were being sacrificed in Spangler's Meadow, Brigadier General Henry Lockwood's brigade attacked from the left of the springs, ran past them, and attacked *Steuart's* entrenched brigade up Culp's Hill in the direction your car is parked. During the engagement, the Federal 1st Maryland (the Potomoc Home Brigade) fought fellow Marylanders in the Confederate 1st Maryland Battalion.

After the battle, many men were buried in the flat ground near the spring. Later, several hundred wounded horses were gathered up on the battlefield, led to the field across the park road from Spangler Spring, and shot. For many years, their bones lay in a thicket on the north side of the little creek that runs down into Rock Creek.

➤ Continue along the road you are on (Slocum Avenue) until you reach Tour Stop 14.

☛ **ALONG THE WAY TO TOUR STOP 14.** As you drive up Culp's Hill from Spangler's Spring, you pass the sites of intense fighting between the two forces during the evening of July 2 and again the next morning. Wave after wave of infantry from *Johnson's* division were recklessly thrown against entrenched Union troops. This road follows the defensive line. To the right side of the road are the remains of breastworks thrown up by the Union forces on the night of July 1. The Confederates were attacking from your right to your left.

One of the monuments on the right commemorates the 1st Maryland Battalion. This first Confederate memorial's placement was full of controversy. For example, the unit's designation had to be changed from its actual 1st Maryland to the 2d Maryland to avoid confusion with Union regiments of the same designation. A part of *Steuart's* brigade, it helped capture some of the Union breastworks on July 2. The next day, the regiment advanced an additional 100 yards before being forced back. There is a small marker designating this spot in the woods to the left of the road where it intersects with another (Geary Avenue) coming in from the left.

The monument to the 149th New York is farther along on your right. It contains a bronze plaque portraying how its flag bearer mended the unit's flagstaff during the height of the battle. At the conclusion of the fight, the flag had more than eighty bullet holes in it.

You may stop and climb the observation tower on Culp's Hill, which gives a good view of the area. Nearby is the monument to Greene, whose small brigade valiantly held this hill on the evening of July 2 after the rest of the XII Corps was sent to help fight off *Longstreet*. Remains of breastworks constructed during the evening of July 1 run along the trail to the left of Greene's monument. So desperate was the fighting here that the Confederate dead and wounded lay in heaps.

TOUR STOP 14. STEVEN'S KNOLL. (SEE P. 89)

(See p. 89)

This high ground bridges Cemetery Hill in front of you with Culp's Hill behind you. The stop contains a monument to Major General Henry Slocum, commander of the XII Corps, and a memorial to Steven's battery, which was positioned here. The latter was called the Iron Brigade Battery, and it inflicted heavy losses on Confederate infantry during the first day of the battle when it was positioned on Seminary Ridge. Here the guns sit where they were on the evening of July 2, when they tried to thwart a Confederate attack on Cemetery Hill, in front of you.

> We will not follow the signs for the park route now. After driving for about a block, you see the sign for the auto tour. Ignore it and bear to your right, onto Wainwright Avenue.

As you drive along this narrow road, you see East Cemetery Hill on your left. During the evening of July 1, remnants of the Union army took refuge on this hill and built breastworks. The Confederates chose not to attack until the evening of July 2, when two of *Early's* brigades hit this hill from beyond the woods in your right-front. Although the hill was considered impregnable, these two brigades charged up its slope through tremendous artillery fire that blew holes in the ranks. Driving the Federal infantry off the hill, *Early's* men turned to the cannon placed here. The cannoneers refused to give up their guns without a fight and engaged in hand-to-hand combat before being driven from their guns. Federal infantry now converged from three directions, forcing *Early's* men back off the hill. It was so dark by this time that the Union reinforcements could find the area only by seeing the flashes from the guns of *Early's* men. You may see the memorials to Howard and Major General Winfield Scott Hancock, both on horseback, on the hill.

➤ Continue on this road until you reach a stop sign. Turn left here onto Lefever Street and go one block to Baltimore Pike. Carefully, make another left turn onto Baltimore Pike. Bear left at the light. You might wish to park near Evergreen Cemetery and walk across the road to the crest of East Cemetery Hill, which was briefly captured by *Early's* men. Continue on Baltimore Pike and turn right onto Hunt Avenue (8.2 miles from Little Round Top). When this road dead-ends, make a left onto Taneytown Road and, when you see a sign for the auto tour,

Cemetery Hill, looking toward Culp's Hill. Reynolds's battery, which participated in attempting to stop Early's attack on July 2, is in the foreground. Beyond the tent you can see some of the entrenchments thrown up by the men of Wadsworth's division during the battle. In the background is the heavily wooded Culp's Hill.

make a right turn onto Pleasonton Avenue (9.2 miles from Little Round Top). When Pleasonton Avenue dead-ends, make a right onto Hancock Avenue and drive to Tour Stop 15.

☛ **ALONG THE WAY TO TOUR STOP 15.** As you get back onto Hancock Avenue, you will see on your left the position of the Union battle line charged with stopping *Pickett's* Charge. The most important landmark was the "copse of trees," now encircled with a fence. *Pickett's* men used this as a target as they approached Cemetery Ridge on the afternoon of July 3.

Two monuments on your right commemorate the role of the Vermont troops in this sector. The 13th Vermont led a fierce counterattack during the early evening of July 2 that pushed *Wright's* brigade off Cemetery Ridge after the Georgians pierced the Union line. The next day, the 13th and 16th Vermont attacked *Kemper's* brigade, the right-most unit of *Pickett's* division, and materially assisted in repulsing the Virginians. If you look closely at Lieutenant Stephen Brown's right foot, you see a hatchet. Brown had been

Modern view. The park has become more heavily wooded since the battle. This view is from the Evergreen Cemetery Gatehouse between Tour Stops 14 and 15.

arrested before the battle for a petty infraction and his sword had been taken from him. He was permitted to rejoin his men during the battle and, without a sword (the monument is inaccurate), he picked up a hatchet and used it to lead his men. A number of other interesting monuments are in this area, including an undressed granite boulder commemorating the 20th Massachusetts that sits far back on the left side of the road. Transported from a playground in Massachusetts, it conveys the meaning that men who once played as children fought so gallantly here at Gettysburg. The monument with the Native American on the right side of the road commemorates the 42d New York, or the Tammany Regiment, which was raised and supported by the political machine in New York City. The group took its name from Chief Tamenend, who led the Delaware tribe at the time Pennsylvania was colonized.

TOUR STOP 15. HIGH WATER MARK. (SEE P. 102)

During the afternoon of July 3, this area was a maelstrom of bullets, cannon fire, and dead and dying men and horses as *Pickett's* men attacked. Park your car, walk to the copse of trees on the left side of the road, and observe Seminary Ridge, about three-quarters of a mile in front of you on the other side of Emmitsburg Road. You may be able to see the Virginia Memorial in the distance where *Lee* anxiously watched the charge. *Pickett's* men crossed these open fields in tight formation, only to be devastated by converging cannon and small-arms fire. This sector was defended by the Philadelphia Brigade. To your right is the Angle, through which *Brigadier General Lewis Armistead* led his men while twirling his hat on his sword. A memorial to where he was mortally wounded lies to the right of the copse.

In front of you and to your left sits the Codori House on Emmitsburg Road, where *Pickett* watched in anguish as his troops were destroyed. The cover painting illustrates what happened at the point where you are standing. To your far right, the men of *Trimble's* and *Pettigrew's* divisions were also charging up this ridge.

Of the 4,500 men that *Pickett* took into the charge, only about 200 made it over the wall in front of you to engage the Philadelphia Brigade in hand-to-hand combat. They threw back the Union line, but converging units from the left and right rapidly repaired the breach. Only about one-third of *Pickett's* troops returned to Seminary Ridge unharmed.

The High Water Mark of the Confederacy. This photograph shows the low stone wall defended by the Philadelphia Brigade. The statue on the right honors one of its regiments. Pickett's division began their charge on Seminary Ridge, which can be discerned by the Virginia Memorial in the background. General Pickett watched the charge from the Codori House, which is to the left of the photograph.

Several monuments attempt to capture a sense of the intense fighting here, including that of the 72d Pennsylvania, along the stone wall to the right of the copse of trees. It shows a Fire Zouave of the Philadelphia Brigade swinging the butt of his rifle against *Pickett's* men. *Pickett's* advance against this position obscured an important event the day before, when *Wright's* brigade advanced virtually alone and drove through a gap to the left of the copse of trees. The attack was finally repelled by separate charges of the 13th Vermont to the left of you and by the 106th Pennsylvania to the right of the copse of trees. The bronze base relief on the 106th Pennsylvania monument shows the charge against the Codori farm on July 2, when the regiment pushed *Wright* back toward Seminary Ridge.

You may walk on the High Water Mark Trail, which takes you to Meade's headquarters at the Leister farmhouse.

> Continue along Hancock Road and turn left onto the service road, then right onto Steinwehr Avenue. Reenter the visitor center parking lot on your right. Park and cross the road to the National Cemetery.

(☛ **ALONG THE WAY TO TOUR STOP 16.** As you drive northward along Hancock Avenue, you pass over the ground that *Trimble's* and *Pettigrew's* men were attempting to capture. The ground around the 1st Delaware's monument on the left side of the road was the scene of intense fighting. This regiment, along with the 125th New York, whose monument is ahead to the right of the road, charged into *Pettigrew's* flank, driving it back with heavy losses.

The Bryan House, home of a freed slave at the time of the battle, sits on the right side of the road.

TOUR STOP 16. NATIONAL CEMETERY.

Cemetery Hill is important for several reasons. First, it had great strategic value: the army that held it commanded the northern part of the battle-field. For this reason, the hill was heavily fortified by Union troops on the afternoon of July 1. Second, the circular, continuous rows of flat stones mark the resting place for more than 3,600 Union dead. Third, Abraham Lincoln gave his immortal Gettysburg Address at the cemetery's dedication. As you enter the cemetery, you see the Lincoln Speech Memorial on your right, which contains tablets depicting the invitation to Lincoln to speak at the dedication and a copy of his address. Because of a disagreement over where to place the monument, it was never officially dedicated and "temporarily" sits on this site. Near the memorial is a large brick rostrum, built in 1879. Dignitaries, including several presidents, have spoken on this platform on every anniversary of the address.

The site where Lincoln spoke is marked by the Soldiers' Monument, the first monument to be erected on the battlefield. The effort to create a suitable burial place for the dead began soon after the battle ended, when a local attorney, David Wills, was asked to select a site and begin the planning and implementation. A seventeen-acre site was selected and, on November 19, 1863, the National Cemetery was dedicated. Though only Union soldiers were to be buried here, some Confederates probably were also mistakenly interred here as well. Near the fence is the monument to the 1st U.S. Artillery. One of the guns was made by the company founded by Paul Revere.

OPTIONAL TOUR STOPS

OPTIONAL TOUR STOP A. BARLOW'S KNOLL.

➤ At Tour Stop 3, set your trip odometer and turn left on the road just beyond the tower parking lot. This takes you back to Mummasburg Road. Make a right onto Mummasburg Road and drive 0.5 mile from the tower to Howard Avenue on your left. Turn into it and continue east to Barlow's Knoll after crossing Carlisle Road.

☛ **ALONG THE WAY TO Optional TOUR STOP A.** As you turn onto Howard Avenue, you trace the line held by Brigadier General Alexander Schimmelfennig's brigade of the XI corps. Most of the men of this corps were German immigrants, many of whom could not speak English. Not known for their fighting prowess, these men had fled before the enemy two months before at the Battle of Chancellorsville and fled again at Gettysburg.

OPTIONAL TOUR STOP A. BARLOW'S KNOLL.

Face the flagpole (north). Brigadier General Francis Barlow's division occupied the fields to your left and right. For some reason, Barlow positioned his division here, far in advance of Schimmelfennig's division, whose unit markers you passed before you crossed Carlisle Road. This left Barlow vulnerable to attack. As *Heth's*, *Pender's* and *Rodes's* divisions were pounding the I Corps, *Early's* division of *Ewell's* II Corps arrived along Harrisburg Road and deployed in the fields in front of you. *Gordon's* brigade moved slowly forward from a position in front of you, while *Doles'* brigade of *Rodes's* division moved against the knoll from your left. Hit in two directions, Barlow's position was untenable, and the men fell back in disorder toward Gettysburg. Barlow himself was seriously wounded. Many of Barlow's men were captured as they retreated.

Getting Back to the Regular Tour and Tour Stop 4. We will not follow the park service's auto route to return to the main tour. Retrace your steps to Mummasburg Road. Turn right onto Mummasburg Road and make a left onto Robinson Road, just on the opposite side of the railroad tracks. Make a left at the stop sign at the top of the hill and you are back on the main tour.

OPTIONAL TOUR STOP B. EAST CAVALRY FIELD.

➤ From the Gettysburg visitor center, make a left onto Washington Avenue and drive to York Street. Turn right and drive around the circle, staying on York Street on the other side. The road forks; take the one on your left. About 4.1 miles from the visitor center (after you cross Route 15) you will see Cavalry Field Road on your right. There are no special signs marking this road. Turn into it and continue until it makes a sharp bend to the right. You will soon see markers and monuments.

OPTIONAL TOUR STOP B. EAST CAVALRY FIELD.

A s *Pickett's* men attacked Cemetery Ridge on July 3, *Major General J.E.B. Stuart's* cavalry was ordered to attack the ridge from its rear. As he made his wide flanking movement to the west of town, he was confronted by Union cavalry under Major General Alfred Pleasonton. Monuments show you where the various brigades stood on the afternoon of the third day, where *Stuart* launched his attack against the Federal cavalry, and the location of the countercharge of Brigadier General George Custer's brigade.

➤ Turn around and retrace your route to return to Gettysburg.

OPTIONAL TOUR STOP C. THE TOWN OF GETTYSBURG.

➤ Begin at the visitor center and turn left out of the parking lot, onto Washington Avenue. At the light, turn right onto Steinwehr Avenue, which flows into Baltimore Street at the next light. Turn right here and, within a block, you see the Jenny Wade House on your left. Pull into the parking lot next to it.

OPTIONAL TOUR STOP C. TOWN OF GETTYSBURG.

Jenny Wade was the only civilian killed during the battle. Baking bread for the Union troops stationed nearby, she was killed when a bullet passed through two doors and lodged in her back during the morning of July 3. You may visit the museum and gift shop here or continue with the tour.

> Turn right onto Baltimore Pike and continue to the Town Square.

As you approach the Town Square, you see the old Hotel Gettysburg, which was used as a hospital during the battle, directly in front of you. Directly to your right as you enter the square is a statue of Lincoln. This was the house of David Wills, the man charged with designing the National Cemetery. Lincoln stayed here, and it is said that he completed his address in this home.

> Continue around the square and enter Carlisle Street, directly across from Baltimore Street.

At the end of the first block, you cross railroad tracks. To your right is the train station where Lincoln disembarked to assist in dedicating the cemetery. The building is now the Gettysburg Information Center.

> Continue north to Stevens Street, where you will turn right. Drive through the intersection with Stratton Street. When you come to the dead-end, carefully make a U-turn and park on the right.

On the side of the building you will see a mural depicting the desperate fight between Colonel Charles Coster's brigade and *Early's* division on July 1. Sent down from their reserve position on Cemetery Hill, Coster's men were ordered to stop the Confederate advance in this vicinity, but instead were pushed back to their former positions with heavy losses.

> Turn left onto Stratton and drive south to York Street (Route 116).

At the intersection with York Street is St. James Lutheran Church, a large building that was used as a hospital during and after the battle.

> Cross York Street and turn left onto Middle Street. This will take you back to the visitor center.

PART II

NARRATIVE
OF THE BATTLE

WHY WAS THE BATTLE FOUGHT?
WHY AT GETTYSBURG?

The future of the Confederacy looked grim in the spring of 1863. Union armies controlled large sections of the South's heartland, including a number of vital ports such as New Orleans, Louisiana; Memphis, Tennessee; and Norfolk, Virginia. A vital point on the Mississippi River—Vicksburg, Mississippi—was under siege, and a strong blockade of other ports was squeezing the South.

The only bright spot for the South was *General Robert E. Lee* and his Army of Northern Virginia. Time and again, they had defeated better-equipped and numerically superior Union armies in bloody battles in Virginia. Most recently, with about a third of his army absent, *Lee* had utterly routed the Army of the Potomac under Major General Joseph Hooker at the Battle of Chancellorsville. Despite these successes, the South was slowly bleeding to death, and *Lee* realized that the only hope for the Confederacy was a bold strike into the North that would throw fear into the citizens and cause them to clamor for peace.

There were other reasons for the invasion. An incursion into the fat farmlands of Maryland and Pennsylvania would provide much-needed food and clothing. After more than two years of war, Virginia's resources were being rapidly depleted, so it was time to move north and exploit the Union's abundance. Such a bold move would not only draw the Federal army away from Richmond, it could threaten Washington. This might ease pressure on

Vicksburg if the Federal leadership were forced to transfer troops to protect its capital. If Washington fell, vast stores of supplies would fall into Rebel hands. Finally, a victory in the North might also clinch European recognition of the Confederacy and force the Union to sue for peace.

This would not be the first time that *Lee* had ventured north. Barely eight months before, his army had gotten to within twenty miles of the Pennsylvania line when it was forced to turn and do battle. Though again outnumbered, *Lee* fought the Army of the Potomac to a standoff at the Battle of Antietam, in what remains America's bloodiest day of fighting, September 17, 1862. Crippled by this action, *Lee's* army limped back to Virginia to recover.

LEE'S PLAN

Lee spent several months planning the second invasion of the North, having ordered maps of Maryland and Pennsylvania in February 1863. Not all of the authorities in Richmond shared his enthusiasm. Some felt that *Lee* and some of his troops should be shifted west, where they could join another powerful Confederate army and invade Kentucky and Ohio. In the end, *Lee* prevailed, and he set about stripping the South of as many troops as he could. For once, he would fight with almost equal strength.

Lee's resounding victory over Hooker at Chancellorsville in May 1863 reinforced two impressions: Union commanders were easily cowed and bluffed by the Army of the Northern Virginia, and *Lee's* own men were "invincible." The Confederates were bedraggled but well armed and tough fighters. Man for man, *Lee's* army may have been the finest fighting force ever assembled by this country. Because of these factors, *Lee* felt that he could take giant risks—a conclusion that would bring him grief at Gettysburg. Shortly after Chancellorsville, he put his new plan into effect.

Slipping around the Army of the Potomac's right flank, *Lee's* army would cross through the Blue Ridge passes into the Shenandoah Valley that stretches from Virginia into Pennsylvania. Screened by mountains on both sides, the Southern army would move quickly into Maryland and Pennsylvania. After defeating the Northern army, *Lee* planned to swoop down on Washington or Baltimore and demand peace.

Although Chancellorsville was perhaps *Lee's* greatest victory, it may have ultimately contributed to his defeat at Gettysburg. During this battle, his most successful and dependable subordinate, *Lieutenant General Thomas J. Jackson*, was mortally wounded. *Lee* subsequently reorganized his army into three corps. The first was lead by a veteran commander, *Lieu-*

tenant General James Longstreet. The other two were commanded by men new to their posts. *Lieutenant General Richard Ewell*, newly returned to the army after recovering from the loss of a leg at the Battle of Second Manassas, led the II Corps. *Lieutenant General Ambrose Powell Hill*, a man with much potential but who suffered from mysterious ailments, led the III Corps. *Lee* thus ventured forth on his most important campaign with two untried corps commanders. This decision proved disastrous.

During early June 1863, the two great armies warily faced each other on opposite sides of the Rappahannock River at Fredericksburg, Virginia. Each stood in the path of the other's drive toward the enemy's capital. Facing *Lee* were the 95,000 battle-hardened veterans of the Army of the Potomac. These men had long suffered under poor leadership and had therefore lost more than their share of battles. The army was composed of seven corps (I, II, III, V, VI, XI, XII) whose individual commanders were nonetheless quite competent for the most part.

Both armies shared a common organization: corps were composed of divisions (usually three) that were composed of two to four brigades. Each brigade contained four to six regiments that usually numbered 200 to 400 men each. There were fewer Confederate corps and divisions, but each unit tended to be larger than their Union counterparts.

THE CONFEDERATES START NORTH

The invasion began when *Longstreet's* corps quietly slipped away from its position on June 3 and moved west to Culpeper Court House. *Ewell* followed within two days (see Map 1, p. 40). After resting there for about a week, *Ewell* slipped through the mountain passes and entered the Shenandoah Valley, then marched quickly northward. *Longstreet* was to first bluff Hooker into thinking that an attack on Washington was imminent, then cut through the Blue Ridge at Snicker's Gap and enter the Valley. *Hill* remained at Fredericksburg to block Hooker along the Rappahannock. Hooker could have decided to strike at Richmond, since two-thirds of the Southern army had slipped away. *Hill* was to immediately follow *Ewell* and *Longstreet* if Hooker began to move northward.

After hearing of Confederate columns moving to his right, Hooker ordered Major General Alfred Pleasonton, with 8,000 cavalry and 3,000 infantry, to march to Culpeper to learn more about the status of *Lee's* army. Pleasonton fell on Confederate cavalry at Brandy Station on June 8 and one of the great cavalry battles of the war ensued. While *Major General J.E.B.*

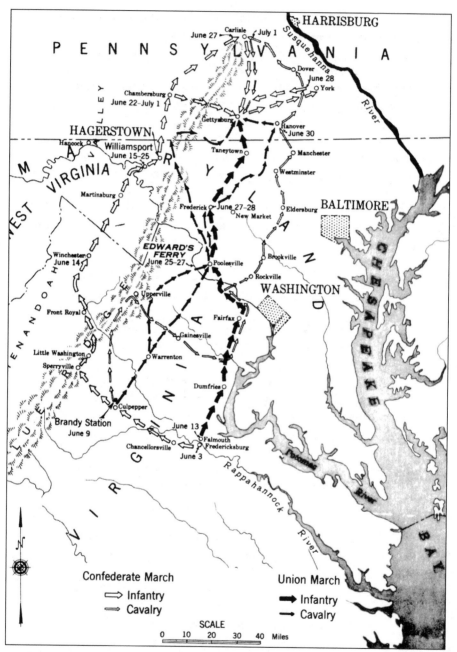

Map 1. Strategy: the march to Gettysburg.

Stuart's cavalrymen pushed Pleasonton back with heavy losses, the Northerners had, for the first time, acquitted themselves well in a fight with the more experienced Southern horsemen. Union cavalry later tangled with its Confederate counterparts at the important Blue Ridge passes at Upperville, Aldie, and Middleburg, Virginia, as Pleasonton aggressively sought out the enemy's location.

Upon arriving in the northern Shenandoah Valley, *Ewell* fell on 9,000 Federal troops slowly retreating toward Washington. While distracting the Northerners, a division of infantry under *Major General Edward Johnson* slipped behind them. When the Battle of Winchester was over, only 4,000 Union troops made it to safety. *Ewell's* men also captured twenty-three cannon and 200,000 rounds of small-arms ammunition. Confederate spirits soared at this development. *Ewell* quickly crossed into Maryland and Pennsylvania. After halting at Chambersburg, *Lee* ordered *Ewell* to capture Harrisburg, the capital of Pennsylvania.

Ewell detached his three divisions. One under *Major General Jubal Early* collected supplies at Gettysburg, then marched on York, ultimately capturing and ransoming it for $28,600, 1,000 hats, 1,000 pairs of socks, 1,500 pairs of shoes, and 1,500 pairs of boots. *Early* then was ordered to cross the Susquehanna River, capture Lancaster, then move on Harrisburg from the north. *Ewell's* second division, under *Major General Robert Rodes*, reached Carlisle, west of Harrisburg, on June 27, and remained there for about three days before marching toward Harrisburg. *Ewell's* third division, *Johnson's*, aimed directly for Harrisburg.

At one stage of the campaign, *Lee's* column was greatly attenuated, with its head nearing the Susquehanna and its tail south of the Potomac River. Piecing together intelligence reports, President Abraham Lincoln deduced that the Southern army was stretched out over a 95-mile span. Realizing that "the animal must be pretty slim somewhere in the middle," he suggested that Hooker find a way to attack it. At the very least, he ordered Hooker to position his army between *Lee's* hoard and the capital. At the same time, Lincoln issued an urgent call for militia men. Before long, 15,000 poorly trained men streamed toward Harrisburg.

By June 24, all of *Lee's* troops were across the Potomac, but amazingly, the entire Union army remained in Virginia. Hooker refused to move until the enemy "developed his intentions." Finally realizing that the Southern army could get between the Army of the Potomac and Washington, Hooker ordered forced marches. Hikes of twenty, thirty, and even thirty-five miles in a twenty-four-hour period were common. Hundreds of men fell from the ranks suffering from heat stroke. By June 27, the last of Hooker's men were across the Potomac and, by the next day, were concentrated in central Maryland.

While the Union army remained far to the south on June 28, *Hill's* and *Longstreet's* six divisions had already crossed the Pennsylvania line and occupied Chambersburg. *Ewell's* divisions were farther north, near Harrisburg. *Lee* established his headquarters just east of Chambersburg. While there, he issued General Order No. 72, which prohibited harming private property. Anything taken was to be paid for with Confederate script.

The cavalry was the eyes and ears of the armies. *Lee* ordered *Stuart* to ride along the west side of the mountains, screening the movement of the infantry, and keep track of Federal movements. But the orders were vague and *Stuart* interpreted them to permit another adventuresome jaunt around the Union army. He had done this twice before with positive results. As a result, the Southern cavalry was out of touch with *Lee* and didn't know where the main Federal columns were. *Stuart* couldn't get what information he did collect to *Lee*. As a result, *Lee* was ignorant of the Union army's position for much of the campaign.

Lee still intended to concentrate at or near Harrisburg. On the night of June 28, however, he received word that a spy in *Longstreet's* employ had reported two startling developments. The Federal army was not in Virginia, as *Lee* had supposed, but near Frederick, Maryland, and because of forced marches, it was rapidly approaching. To make matters worse, the Army of the Potomac was now commanded by Major General George Meade. *Lee* knew Meade to be a competent if colorless commander and is quoted as having said, "He will commit no blunder in my front, and if I make one, he will make haste to take advantage of it." *Lee* could not have known how prophetic his words were. His army was scattered and unless immediately concentrated, it could be defeated piecemeal by the advancing Federal troops.

LEE CHANGES HIS PLAN

Lee immediately ordered his corps commanders to march on Cashtown, the eastern exit of the pass through South Mountain, eight miles west of Gettysburg. It was difficult for *Ewell*, poised to capture Harrisburg, to disengage. Indeed, a cavalry detachment was within two miles of the city. The Rebel scare had already spread; earthworks were being thrown up around Philadelphia and valuables from New York City were being moved to safety.

Lee's choice of the Cashtown area as the concentration point was made to ensure that the upcoming battle would occur east of the Blue Ridge Mountains. This would give *Lee* room to maneuver and ensure his supply line in Virginia. If Meade were defeated, the area would be a good starting point for a new advance against important strategic objectives in Northern territory. Conversely, if his own army were defeated, the mountains would aid his withdrawal into Virginia.

MEADE SUCCEEDS HOOKER

Lincoln realized that "Fighting Joe" Hooker had to be replaced as commander of the Army of the Potomac. Not only had his officers and men lost confidence in him, it was clear that he was not up to the task of expelling *Lee* from Northern soil. But politics played an important part in military decisions, so Lincoln could not easily remove him from command. It would be much easier for Hooker to resign.

As with most of the commanders of the Army of the Potomac, Hooker wildly overestimated the strength of the Confederate army. After repeatedly requesting the transfer of the troops at Harper's Ferry, West Virginia, and being denied, plus realizing that *Lee* posed a real threat to the North, Hooker decided to call it quits. Lincoln quickly accepted his resignation and immediately began a search for a replacement. There were plenty of candidates but he wanted someone who would listen to his advice and also aggressively take on *Lee*.

Lincoln's first choice was Major General John Reynolds, who held the highest seniority. Reynolds said that he would accept the post only if he was permitted to direct the army as he saw fit. This demand was unacceptable to Lincoln, so he settled on another Pennsylvanian, Meade. Sound asleep in his tent at 2 A.M. on June 28, Meade was awakened by a messenger with an order to take over command of the army. After protesting that others were far more worthy, he was quoted as saying, "Well, I've been tried and condemned without a hearing, and I suppose I shall have to go to execution." Forty-seven years old, the tall and balding Meade often despaired of not having the political connections to advance in the army, though his was a prominent Philadelphia family.

The choice was a good one. Unlike the previous army commanders, Meade had a normal-sized ego and was not averse to following Lincoln's desires. More important, he was a veteran whom the men respected. He knew how to fight, which was shown at Gettysburg.

So disorganized was the army that the new commanding general only generally knew where his seven corps and *Lee's* three were. Meade found himself catapulted without warning into a supremely responsible position in the presence of a powerful invading army, and without a plan.

The army was scattered over a thirty–mile strip in Maryland, with one end at the Potomac River and the other at Middletown, west of Frederick. His instructions from Washington allowed him complete freedom to maneuver and fight, so long as he covered the approaches to Washington and Baltimore. General in Chief Henry W. Halleck's emphasis on protecting these cities, coupled with Meade's inadequate information as to *Lee's* whereabouts and intentions, forced the Federal commander to adopt a defensive strategy.

This was a particularly stressful time for Meade. The defeat of his army on Northern soil would probably result in the loss of Baltimore, Washington, or even Philadelphia, and the political backlash could well result in independence for the Confederacy. Selecting a potential line of defense along Big Pipe Creek, several miles northwest of Westminster, Maryland, and twenty miles southeast of Gettysburg, he first pulled his far-flung corps toward Frederick before sending them cautiously northward on a broad front. He intended to halt *Lee's* advance and bring his army to battle at a time and place yet to be determined.

At this stage of the campaign, neither *Lee* nor Meade had thought much of Gettysburg. Each expected to occupy a strong defensive position and compel his opponent to attack. Nevertheless, the troops of both armies were marching on the ten roads that converged at Gettysburg, so it was only a matter of time before their advance elements collided at this town.

ADVANCE TO CONTACT

On June 30 and July 1, Meade's seven corps marched in parallel columns north from the Frederick area (See Map 1, page 40). Three advanced on the direct route from Frederick to Gettysburg by way of Emmitsburg, Maryland—Reynolds's I, Oliver Howard's XI, and Daniel Sickles's III, in that order. The four other corps were also on the move: Major General Winfield Hancock's II Corps was advancing toward Taneytown; from Uniontown, Maryland, General Henry Slocum's XII Corps was advancing toward Littlestown, Pennsylvania; Major General George Sykes's V Corps was moving north from Westminster, Maryland, to Hanover, Pennsylvania; and Major General John Sedgwick's VI Corps was moving from Manchester, east to Westminster, north toward Gettysburg.

On the night before the battle began, the I Corps bivouacked along Marsh Creek, five miles south of Gettysburg, with the XI Corps at Emmitsburg, four miles farther south. Both had orders to advance to Gettysburg the following day. Brigadier General John Buford's cavalry had already arrived in Gettysburg, and he periodically sent back messages about *Lee's* movements.

That night, more than 70,000 troops were bivouacked within ten miles of Gettysburg—27,000 Union infantry of the I and XI Corps, artillery, and cavalry; and 43,000 Confederate infantry (23,000 men of *A. P. Hill's* III Corps and 14,000 men of *Longstreet's* I Corps) and artillery, with a scattering of cavalry on Chambersburg Pike on its way to the rendezvous at Cashtown. Leading this column was *Major General Henry Heth's* division of *Hill's* corps.

Two of *Longstreet's* divisions commanded by *Major Generals Lafayette McLaws* and *John Bell Hood* brought up the rear. *Longstreet's* remaining division, under *Major General George Pickett*, was left at Chambersburg to protect the wagon trains and the army's rear. *Hood* and *McLaws* were seriously delayed near Greenwood when *Major General Edward Johnson's* division of *Ewell's* II Corps cut into the column on Chambersburg Pike. *Johnson* had been marching south from Carlisle toward Chambersburg when he received *Lee's* message to rendezvous at Cashtown. Taking a shortcut below Shippensburg, he turned onto the pike just as *Longstreet's* men were about to pass. The latter's troops were ordered to give way to *Johnson's* men as well as to *Johnson's* and *Rodes's* supply trains. This column covered fifteen miles of road, forcing *Longstreet* to delay his march by six hours or more.

While seven Confederate divisions were strung out along the road between Chambersburg and Gettysburg approaching the town from the west, other Confederate columns were converging on Gettysburg from the north. A part of *Rodes's* division had reached Biglerville, less than ten miles north of Gettysburg, while *Early's* division was moving rapidly along the roads leading from Harrisburg, Carlisle, and York.

Initial contact between the two armies was made on the afternoon of June 30, when elements of *Pettigrew's* brigade of *Heth's* division collided with Buford's cavalry pickets just west of Gettysburg. Not knowing the strength of the enemy, *Pettigrew* wisely withdrew and bivouacked for the night along Marsh Creek. Here *Heth's* division was joined by another of *Hill's* divisions under *Major General Dorsey Pender*.

While Meade established his headquarters at Taneytown, Maryland, fifteen miles southeast of Gettysburg, *Lee* advanced with his troops from Chambersburg on June 30 on the road to Cashtown and spent the night at Greenwood, ten miles east of Chambersburg. Upon reaching Cashtown on the morning of July 1, *Lee* could hear the sounds of battle up ahead in the distance. He soon found a sick *Hill*, who was unable to tell him what was happening, so he galloped on to find out for himself and to take command. Never before had *Lee* been so completely in the dark at so critical a moment.

Lee was determined not to bring on a general engagement until his army was fully reassembled and he could learn more definitely about the strength, location, and intent of the Union army. Positive orders to that effect had been issued to his corps commanders but they were not obeyed.

THE FIRST DAY'S BATTLE

CHAMBERSBURG PIKE AT WILLOUGHBY RUN
5:20 A.M., JULY 1, 1863

Buford's cavalry had screened the left front and flank of Meade's army during its advance northward. It arrived in Gettysburg on June 30, just in time to encounter the scouts of *Pettigrew's* brigade of *Heth's* division marching from Cashtown. *Pettigrew* had been sent ahead to seize shoes and other supplies reported to be in Gettysburg. Instead of running into local militia, as expected, *Pettigrew* encountered a strong force of Union cavalry and prudently withdrew back toward Cashtown.

Confident that the Confederates would return in force the next day, Buford spread his dismounted cavalry to the west and north of the town. Colonel William Gamble's brigade was assigned to the east of Chambersburg Pike; Thomas Devin's, to the north and northwest.

Buford's men were good dismounted fighters, who used their horses merely as a quick ride to the front. When combat was imminent, the men would dismount and one man in four held the horses in the rear while the others fought as infantry. The horses were quickly brought up when it was time to advance or retire. The men carried seven-shot Spencer repeating carbines that replaced their old single-shot rifles. As a result, Buford's two brigades had the firepower of almost three times their number.

Shortly after 6:00 A.M. on July 1, Buford's picket line could see a cloud of dust in the distance. The troopers knew it was Rebel infantry and lots of it. On the Confederates came until, at 7:30 A.M., they were close enough to be fired on. The first shot of the battle was fired by Lieutenant Marcellus Jones of the 8th Illinois Cavalry, who aimed at a mounted officer but missed.

ACTION OF BUFORD'S CAVALRY
8:00 TO 10:00 A.M., JULY 1

Upon returning from his foraging expedition the day before, *Pettigrew* told *Heth* and *Hill* that regular troops defended Gettysburg, not militia, as had been widely reported. They refused to believe him, and *Heth* asked to take his entire division toward Gettysburg the next day to capture supplies. *Hill* consented and, before dawn, 7,000 veteran infantrymen were marching for the town and a collision with Buford. *Heth* was later accused of recklessness and poor judgment in throwing his entire division forward without an adequate reconnaissance.

At 8:00 A.M., the head of *Heth's* column approached Herr Ridge. Waiting for them were elements of Gamble's brigade and a six-gun battery. Bringing up two batteries, the Confederates moved slowly forward and gradually pushed the cavalrymen back toward McPherson's Ridge. *Heth* then deployed his two lead brigades for action. *Brigadier General James Archer* moved forward to the right of Chambersburg Pike; *Brigadier General Joseph Davis* to the left of it. As the skirmishers advanced, they continued to push Buford's men before them. *Heth's* other two brigades, under *Pettigrew* and *Colonel John Brockenbrough*, were still in the rear. At 9:30, *Archer's* and *Davis's* brigades, totaling 3,500 men and supported by twenty guns, moved toward McPherson's Ridge, where Buford had deployed Gamble's 1,700 men, one regiment from Devin's brigade, and six cannon (See Map 3). Gamble was outnumbered by almost 50 percent, and when *Heth's* remaining 3,500 infantry arrived, the disparity would increase to almost four to one. To make matters worse, Buford was forced to spread his men thinly over an extended front. Nevertheless, his cavalrymen held a good position and had the firepower of almost 6,000 men.

As the Southerners advanced, the small-arms fire increased. The six Union guns surprisingly held their own against the Confederates' twenty. Buford saw all of this and more from his vantage point in the cupola of the Lutheran Seminary. He could see his men valiantly holding off *Heth's*

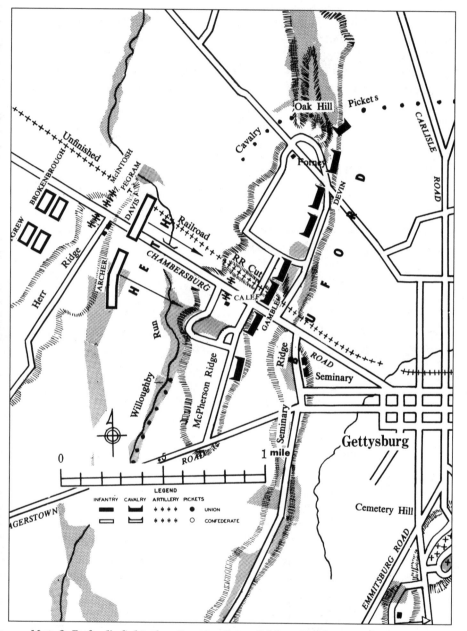

Map 2. Buford's fight: the situation from 8:00 to 10:00 A.M., July 1.

infantry, but to the west, the great columns of dust indicated that additional Rebel troops were on the way. To his dismay, he could see no movement to the south, the direction from which Reynolds's I Corps would be approaching. Buford sent a stream of messengers to Meade and Reynolds, requesting immediate assistance. He considered the hills around Gettysburg to be a fine place to halt the Rebel invasion.

At about 9:45 A.M., Reynolds was seen galloping ahead of his men. Upon reaching the seminary, he conferred with a visibly relieved Buford. After a quick survey, Reynolds realized that the area was as good as any to meet *Lee's* army and sent this message to Meade: "I will fight them inch by inch, and if driven into the town I will barricade the streets and hold them as long as possible." Reynolds rushed his corps toward the firing. He also urged Howard to hurry his XI Corps forward. Before too long, more than 25 percent of the Federal army was taking position in the fields around Gettysburg.

McPherson's Woods
10:15 A.M. to Noon, July .

The I Corps arrived not a moment too soon to keep the Confederates from overrunning Buford's cavalry, seizing the important heights around the town, and defeating Meade's corps as they arrived successively. Throwing off their haversacks, the men of Reynolds's first division under Brigadier General James Wadsworth prepared for action as they approached Buford's troopers. Two regiments of Brigadier General Lysander Cutler's brigade were placed to the south of Chambersburg Pike; the other three were placed north of it. On their left, the storied Iron Brigade ran to its designated positions south of the road as its band played "Yankee Doodle Dandy."

As soon as the Iron Brigade's lead regiment, the 2d Wisconsin, arrived on McPherson's Ridge, it was hit by a tremendous volley from *Archer's* men, who were running up the western slope (See Map 3, p.50). Seeing many men fall and the rest wavering, Reynolds dashed up and yelled, "Forward men, forward, for God's sake, and get those fellows out of those woods!" The men attacked and briefly halted the Southern advance. Turning back to see if reinforcements were coming up, Reynolds was shot in the neck and died instantly. With other units of the Iron Brigade arriving, *Archer's* men were driven back to Willoughby Run, a creek between Herr and McPherson's Ridges.

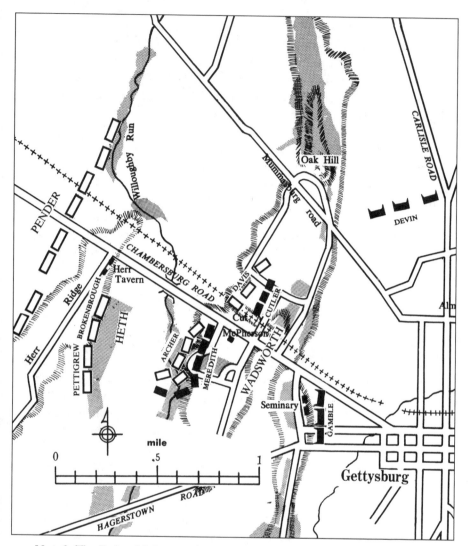

Map 3. The Federal I Corps relieves Buford: the situation from 10:00 A.M. to noon, July 1.

Archer had been warned by *Pettigrew* about the terrain and to be prepared to meet regular troops. He now paid the price for not listening. During this era, units tried to attack the flank and rear of their opponents as a sure way of driving them from the field. Such was the case of the 24th

Michigan of the Iron Brigade, which quietly swept around *Archer's* right flank. While it attacked the Southerners in their flank and rear, the 19th Indiana hit them in the front. The Alabamans had no choice but to flee for their lives. The Yankees bagged seventy-five men, including *Archer*. As *Archer* was marched to the rear, he was met by an old acquaintance from before the war, Major General Abner Doubleday, now commander of the I Corps. Extending his hand, he said, "*Archer*, I am glad to see you!" To this greeting, *Archer* snapped back, "Well, I am not glad to see you, sir," and refused to shake his hand.

It was then fairly easy for the remainder of *Archer's* brigade to be "rolled up" by the Northern troops on their flank and front. By 11:30 A.M., this action was over. The commander of the Iron Brigade, Brigadier General Solomon Meredith, however, could see a large body of Confederates deploying on Herr Ridge, and he wisely pulled his men back to the safety of McPherson's Ridge.

While *Archer's* men were being handled roughly by the Iron Brigade, *Davis's* brigade, advancing north of the road, was having great success against Cutler's brigade (See Map 3, p.50). Here, the 55th North Carolina overlapped Cutler's right flank and charged into the 76th New York from the north while other Southern regiments attacked its front. The 76th and the 56th Pennsylvania fought bravely for thirty minutes, but seeing their numbers being decimated, Wadsworth ordered them to retreat to avoid total destruction. A battery, supported by a third regiment of Cutler's brigade, the 147th New York, briefly stopped *Davis's* troops with double loads of canister. *Davis's* men coolly picked off the gunners, though, forcing them to retreat with the loss of a gun. Hopelessly outnumbered and unsupported, the 147th also withdrew after losing more than 75 percent of its men.

The situation was critical for the Federals. While the Iron Brigade was successfully battling *Archer* on the Union left, the right flank was threatened by *Davis*. Just then, the reserve regiment of the Iron Brigade, the 6th Wisconsin, plus two regiments from Cutler's brigade (the 84th and 95th New York) stationed south of the road, wheeled and attacked *Davis*. Suddenly exposed to musket fire in front and flank, the Rebels made a terrible error. Two regiments (the 2d and 42d Mississippi) jumped into an unfinished railroad cut, thinking that it would protect them. But it was a trap, as it served only to corral *Davis's* men being too steep for them to get out. For the Union troops, it would have been like shooting fish in a barrel. Instead, they called for *Davis's* men to surrender. It was an easy choice for many and the trapped Rebels laid down their arms. The rest retreated back to the west side of Willoughby Run. About 225 men and seven officers from *Davis's* brigade were captured at the cut.

It was 11:30 and the battlefield grew quiet as both sides regrouped. The morning belonged to the Union as two of *Heth's* brigades had been mauled. Unaccountably, he had committed only half of his division, whereas bringing up *Pettigrew* and *Brockenbrough* could have over-whelmed the defenders. After the morning's fiasco, *Heth* finally brought forward the two fresh brigades and reorganized *Archer's*. *Davis's* brigade was pulled out of line and left to lick its wounds and collect stragglers. *Pender's* division also began arriving at Herr Ridge.

On the Union side, Wadsworth was realigning his two brigades behind the creek along McPherson's Ridge and was reinforced by Doubleday's last

The Rose Farm. Another view of Confederate dead adjacent to the Rose Woods. The photographer's wagon, in which film often was developed during the war, is in the far left corner of the photograph.

divisions. Two brigades under Brigadier General Thomas Rowley were separated, with one ordered to each end of the line. Colonel Roy Stone's Pennsylvania Bucktail brigade was sent to the right, where its flank abutted the
road; the second brigade under Colonel Chapman Biddle was placed to the
left of the Iron Brigade. The I Corps' last division, under Brigadier General
John Robinson, was held in reserve on Seminary Ridge, near the Lutheran
school.

Around noon, a crusty old Gettysburg native strolled up to the Iron
Brigade. Dressed in a long blue swallow-tailed coat, buff vest, and high silk
hat, he carried an antique Enfield rifle. A War of 1812 veteran, John Burns
had come to help fight off the Southern invaders. His offer was reluctantly
accepted, and he fought side by side with the men of the 7th Wisconsin,
who marveled that a man over seventy years old could have so much spunk
left in him.

*Modern view of the Rose farm. By finding the rocks and other landmarks,
it is fairly easy to see where the bodies fell during the battle.*

While watching the growing Southern hoard to their front, Stone's men did not see a new threat to their flank. *Rodes's* division, one of *Ewell's*, had arrived on Oak Hill to the north and was deploying. The rude awakening arrived as an artillery shell screamed overhead from their right.

Doubleday tapped his reserves to blunt this new threat. Robinson left the seminary, crossed the unfinished railroad, and formed a line north of it. Stone's brigade was also realigned so that the 150th Pennsylvania continued to face *Heth* to the west, while the 143d and the 149th Pennsylvania changed direction to face north and *Rodes's* new threat. The situation looked grim for the I Corps. Though it had beaten back *Heth's* first advance, the corps now faced two Confederate divisions bearing down on it from the north and west.

REINFORCEMENTS STREAM TOWARD GETTYSBURG
NOON TO 2:00 P.M., JULY 1

While the advance elements slugged it out along Chambersburg Pike, tens of thousands of other men in gray and blue were converging on Gettysburg from all points of the compass. The men of *Ewell's* corps streamed south on the roads leading from Carlisle and York. *Rodes* had begun his march that morning at Biglerville, ten miles north of Gettysburg. The division arrived at Keckler's Hill, within sight of the town, shortly before noon. Here it encountered Devin's cavalry brigade blocking Carlisle Road. So aggressive were the cavalrymen that the Confederates had to deploy and fight before they could advance farther.

As *Rodes* approached from the north, assistance for the I Corps arrived in the form of Howard's XI Corps. Doubleday could not be choosy, but he probably wished that it could have been another outfit. The unlucky XI was composed of large numbers of German-born troops, many of whom did not speak English. It had been on Hooker's flank when *Stonewall Jackson* attacked at Chancellorsville. The XI had been routed and since then had been called the "Flying Dutchmen" by the other troops.

The corps had camped the night before at Emmitsburg, Maryland, about ten miles south of Gettysburg. Receiving Reynolds's order, Howard immediately put his men on the march at 8 A.M. Howard trotted ahead to confer with Reynolds only to learn that he had been killed and that Doubleday was in command. Howard, who was senior, took command of the field. Like *Ewell* on the Southern side, Howard had lost an arm in a previous battle, and this too affected his behavior on the battlefield. Deeply religious and jealous

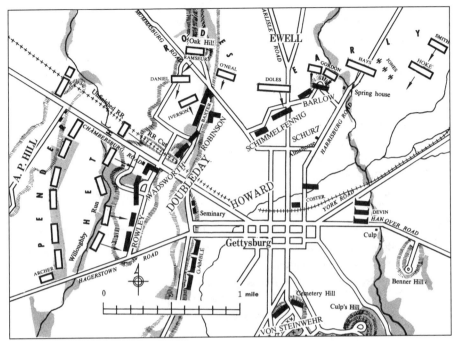

Map 4. Rodes *and* Early *attack, afternoon of July 1.*

of more politically fixed generals, he did not get along well with others. As his three divisions came up, Howard put Major General Carl Schurz in charge of the XI Corps with instructions to place the troops north of Gettysburg. His line was extended to the west, where it was to link at a right angle with the right flank of the I Corps. While the I Corps handled *Hill's* threat from the west, Schurz was directed to halt *Ewell's* corps, approaching from the north and northeast.

Schurz's division, now under Brigadier General Alexander Schimmelfennig, marched through the town about 12:30 P.M., preceded by its German bands. Continuing north on Mummasburg Road, the men were ordered to occupy Oak Hill. They had not gotten far when they realized that the hill was already occupied by *Rodes*, so Howard deployed the troops about 800 yards closer to the town. Schimmelfennig's left rested on Rock Creek and extended toward the northwest. About a half-hour later, another XI division under Brigadier General Francis Barlow marched out of town and entered the fields to the right of Schimmelfennig's division. Barlow was new to command of the division. After Chancellorsville, morale was so low among the men that he had been brought in to whip the division into shape. Rather than forming a continuous line with Schimmelfennig, Barlow continued north, past him, to an exposed position on a wooded knoll that now bears Barlow's name. The movement left a large gap between the divisions. Incredibly, another gap almost a quarter-mile long existed between the I and XI Corps. To have closed this would have put Schimmelfennig's men under intense artillery fire from *Rodes,* so he elected to keep his distance. Not only were both flanks "in the air," but Schurz was stretched so thin that several other gaps opened elsewhere (See Map 4, p. 55). The XI Corps' third division, under Brigadier General Adolph von Steinwehr, was in reserve on Cemetery Hill.

At this point, Howard pleaded to other corps commanders for assistance. Before he was killed, Reynolds had held command over the I, III, and XI corps. The commander of the III Corps, Major General Daniel Sickles, a politician turned general, immediately marched toward Gettysburg in response to Howard's request. Though the XII Corps was only five miles from Gettysburg, its commander, Major General Henry Slocum, a professional soldier, disregarded Howard's pleas, waiting for direct orders from Meade.

FIGHTING ON OAK HILL AND NORTH OF GETTYSBURG
2:00 TO 4:00 P.M., JULY 1

Rodes had immediately deployed his artillery upon his arrival on Oak Hill and opened fire on the right flank of the I Corps. Doubleday reacted by extending his line north and wheeling his flank elements to face more that way. Brigadier General Henry Baxter's brigade of Robinson's division hastened into a partially concealed position behind a stone wall that ran north-south along the east edge of Oak Hill. Cutler's mauled brigade formed on his left. Observing these movements, *Rodes* prepared to attack. Robinson's other brigade, under Brigadier General Gabriel Paul, was nearby, ready to provide support.

Rodes attacked the I Corps from Oak Hill about 1:30 (See Map 4, p. 55). Three of the five Confederate brigades were to push Robinson's flank back toward Gettysburg. *Rodes* had several seasoned brigade commanders, but for some reason selected two relatively untried commanders to spearhead the attack. *O'Neal's* brigade was to move south and hit Robinson's division from the north across Mummasburg Road, while *Iverson's* brigade was to swing around to the west and attack south of the road. At the same time,

Daniel's brigade was to move farther west, find the Union flank, and then drive northward. Caught in a vise, the Union troops would be forced to flee or be captured.

Things went awry from the start. *O'Neal* attacked prematurely and did not coordinate his efforts. He also used just three of his five regiments, and at the wrong point. The brigade shortly was driven back by Baxter with heavy losses.

After *O'Neal's* repulse, *Iverson* attacked on his own without support on either flank. Moving obliquely across an open field, his North Carolinians did not see Baxter's troops crouched behind a stone wall. With *O'Neal's* threat blunted, several of Baxter's regiments jumped to the other side of the wall and faced northwest, to take on *Iverson's* unsuspecting brigade. Its commander elected to watch from the safety of the rear.

Iverson's biggest blunder was in not deploying skirmishers, so his men moved forward as if on parade, oblivious to the threat in front of them. It was certainly a grand spectacle until they approached the stone wall. Suddenly, Baxter's men stood up and delivered a withering volley into *Iverson's* troops. Cutler's brigade sent a deadly crossfire into the Southerners from the south. *Iverson's* men fell in long rows. Many unhurt men also dropped to avoid the hail of bullets. Those foolish enough to try to return fire were quickly hit.

Baxter then pushed out three of his regiments and captured at least 300 prisoners. Out of 1,384 troops that *Iverson* marched into battle, more than 900 were killed, wounded, or captured. One regiment, the 23d North Carolina, lost 89 percent of its men—316 marched in but only thirty-four escaped the ordeal unhurt. One of the survivors later wrote, "Unwarned, unled as a brigade, went forward *Iverson's* deserted band to its doom. Deep and long must the desolate homes and orphan children of North Carolina rue the rashness of that hour." After the battle, *Iverson* was removed from command and reassigned. *O'Neal's* blunder cost him his general's star—the promotion that had been granted before the battle was quickly rescinded after his miserable performance at Gettysburg.

While *Iverson's* men were being sacrificed, another piecemeal attack was launched. *Daniel's* brigade drove down the length of McPherson's Ridge to the right of *Iverson's* men and came to the unfinished railroad cut—the one that had caused so much misery to *Davis's* Mississippians. Stone's Pennsylvania Bucktails were in the cut and delivered an unexpected volley into *Daniel's* approaching troops, throwing them back in confusion. Not content, Stone counterattacked and drove the North Carolinians back even farther. The Confederates regrouped and attacked again, throwing Stone's troops out of the cut. Both sides battled tenaciously, neither willingly giving ground.

As the XI Corps deployed north of town, *Rodes* ordered *Doles's* brigade to attack. Barlow's division, moving to the right of Schimmelfennig's, was hit, but the attack was weak, so the Union line recoiled only slightly.

Because this was an area of open fields, the opposing forces could easily see each other and their dispositions. The Union troops liked what they saw. Because of the repulse of *Rodes's* two center brigades under *Iverson* and *O'Neal, Doles* was unsupported on his right flank. Schimmelfennig exploited this by sending a brigade against *Doles's* flank, but he was prepared for it, and changed his brigade's direction. He barreled into Schimmelfennig and forced the Federals back in confusion. At this juncture, *Doles's* brigade, with fewer than 1,500 men, was up against 5,400 in two of Howard's divisions and faced an attack on its front, flank, and rear. Just then, at about 3:00 P.M., there was movement along Heidlersburg Road. *Major General Jubal Early's* 5,500-man division of *Ewell's* corps had arrived and was quickly deployed in front of the XI Corps.

Early threw *Brigadier General John Gordon's* brigade against Barlow's advanced position at about 3:30 (See Map 4, p.55). *Gordon* advanced slowly to prevent the men from becoming overtired as a result of their long march to the battlefield. They hit Barlow's division from the northeast, while the left regiments of *Doles's* brigade attacked from the northwest. After some sharp hand-to-hand fighting, Barlow was severely wounded and his men broke for the rear. Barlow's replacement, Brigadier General Adelbert Ames, was able to regroup the men, but they were hit again and driven back toward town. On Barlow's left, Schimmelfennig threw Colonel Vladimir Krzyzanowski's brigade against *Doles's* vulnerable right flank. Seeing the danger, *Doles* withdrew briefly, then wheeled his regiments around and, with *Gordon's* help, attacked Schimmelfennig.

Realizing his corps was about to be crushed, Howard needed time to pull back to Cemetery Hill, south of town. He quickly ordered Colonel Charles Coster's brigade (Steinwehr's division) to move down from its reserve perch on Cemetery Hill. Soon after it arrived in a brickyard area, it was attacked by two of *Early's* brigades under *Brigadier Generals Isaac Avery* and *Harry Hays.* After a sharp fight, Coster was swept from the field. One of his regiments, the 154th New York, took 84 percent casualties, mostly through capture.

By 4:00 the XI was a mob, retreating through the streets of Gettysburg. The Confederates followed closely, scooping up thousands of prisoners in the narrow streets. Many avoided capture by hiding. One was Schimmelfennig, who hid in a livestock shed for two days. The shed was later referred to as "Schimmelfennig's Headquarters." Most of the XI Corps finally found haven on Cemetery Hill, where Steinwehr's division and two batteries had been digging in since their arrival several hours before. During this phase of the battle, the XI Corps lost about 3,200 men, or 60 percent of the two divisions engaged. The Confederates lost about 1,000. In a short time, the 6,000 men of the four Confederate brigades north of town had routed 8,000 Union troops in five brigades.

For the first time, the entire Confederate line was moving forward in a coordinated manner. Given this pressure all along the Union line, troops could not be moved around as they were earlier in the battle to thwart the disjointed Confederate advances. It was just a matter of time before the I Corps also broke.

To *Early's* right, Baxter's and Paul's brigades, holding the I Corps' right flank, watched warily as *Rodes* assembled *O'Neal's* and *Ramseur's* men for yet another attack. They were exhausted after fighting for more than three hours in hot weather. With empty canteens and equally empty cartridge boxes, the men wearily fixed bayonets as the Confederate infantry moved steadily forward. At 3:00 P.M., Baxter was told to withdraw and his relieved men streamed southward to safety. Outnumbered two-to-one and without reserves or artillery, Paul's brigade was ordered to occupy Baxter's position and hold the corps' right flank. After sustaining terrible losses from *Ramseur's* and *O'Neal's* attacks but defiantly holding for an hour, it too was permitted to withdraw, leaving behind the 16th Maine to hold back the Confederate tide. The regiment performed admirably but paid the price— out of 275 men that entered the battle, all but forty-three were killed, wounded, or captured. Seeing that its cherished flag was about to be captured, the men ripped it into pieces and distributed them to the survivors.

HETH ATTACKS AGAIN
3:00 P.M., JULY 1

Earlier in the afternoon, while *Rodes* battled the I Corps' right flank, *Heth* fretted. He was ready to resume his own attack on the corps' center and left, but was held back by *Lee*, who was not yet certain that he wanted to bring on a general engagement here. *Heth* won out when he told *Lee* that

Union troops were being moved from his sector to deal with *Rodes*. Finally given orders to attack, *Heth* pushed *Pettigrew's*, *Brockenbrough's*, and *Archer's* brigades forward. The remnants of *Davis's* also advanced with the line. *Pender's* fresh division came up behind these units and prepared to throw its weight into the battle. Just as this formidable line moved forward, *Heth* went down with a bullet to the head. Fortunately for him, the bullet was stopped by a wad of paper placed in the sweat band of his new hat to help it fit better. Nevertheless, he was unconscious for twenty-four hours. The commander of the Iron Brigade, Brigadier General Meredith, was felled about this time by shell fragments.

Heth's brigades moved forward while *Pender's* remained in support. Marching in perfect order, *Pettigrew's* large brigade, which had never been in a battle before, came under a savage artillery fire that blew holes in the ranks. Undaunted, the men continued on until they stood face to face with the Iron Brigade and Biddle's brigade. Volley after volley was fired into each other's ranks. While the Iron Brigade held against *Pettigrew's* left regiments, Biddle could not stem the Southern tide and was forced back. The Confederates then turned to their left and the Iron Brigade was hit in its front and flank. Even it could not sustain such an attack and was forced to retire slowly. On *Pettigrew's* left, *Brockenbrough's* brigade attacked Stone's brigade from the west, while *Daniel* hit it from north of Chambersburg Pike.

Attacked from the west by *Heth* and *Rodes* from the north, the men of the I Corps could take no more. Ammunition was low and Doubleday ordered a withdrawal to Seminary Ridge to the east. As the men fell back, they frequently turned to fire. Once again, Buford's dismounted troopers played an important role in hindering the Confederates. Doubleday's troops deployed on Seminary Ridge fewer in number, but full of fight.

Losses were heavy on both sides. The Iron Brigade had lived up to its name, losing almost three-quarters of its men. Some units lost as many as 80 percent of their strength. The Confederates fared little better. *Iverson's* brigade lost about 65 percent of its men, and one of its units lost almost 90 percent. The fighting had been especially tough on flag-bearers. The 26th North Carolina of *Pettigrew's* brigade lost ten; the 24th of the Iron Brigade, nine. *Heth* entered the battle with about 7,000 men and in twenty-five minutes lost about 2,700.

It was about 4:15 P.M. and *A. P. Hill* called upon *Pender's* division to move through *Heth's* ranks and drive the Yankees off Seminary Ridge. After being pushed from McPherson's Ridge, the thoroughly exhausted remnants of the I Corps took refuge behind stone walls and fences there, and threw up breastworks for one last battle with the advancing Confederates. Three of *Pender's* brigades advanced as if on parade and the Union troops could not help but admire their discipline. As *Pender's* men approached, the I Corps poured volley after volley into them. Behind the I Corps infantry were eighteen cannon, hub to hub, blasting the Rebels with canister. Most of the units stopped in their tracks with heavy losses. *Scales's* brigade, on the left of the line, was decimated by the heavy fire. Repulsed for the first time in the war, this brigade would later muster only 500 men of the 1,400 that entered the battle.

To *Scales's* right, *Colonel Abner Perrin's* South Carolina brigade marched onward with bayonets fixed. The men were not permitted to fire or stop for any reason until the enemy had been ousted from behind the stone wall. The Union fire was devastating. One company of the 14th South Carolina lost thirty-four of its thirty-nine men in one enemy volley. One soldier later wrote, "To stop was destruction, to retreat was disaster, to go forward was orders." The fighting was desperate around the seminary buildings, but finally *Perrin's* men broke through the center of the Union line. Swinging to their right and left, they hurled themselves on the Union flank and rear, forcing the Yankees back off the ridge. Doubleday was neither given the requested assistance of Steinwehr's reserve division on Cemetery Hill nor Howard's permission to retire. Finally, the line could hold no longer and the entire corps was ordered to Cemetery Hill. Units of the I Corps retained their cohesion and occasionally stopped and turned, retarding the Confederate advance. By 5:00 the remnants of the I Corps reached Cemetery Hill and formed on the left of the shattered XI Corps.

The victorious Confederates followed the Union troops toward Gettysburg, scooping up thousands of soldiers. *Perrin's* brigade had the honor of entering Gettysburg first. It and other Confederate units rounded up many Union soldiers who were lost in the maze of streets and alleys. In some cases, almost entire regiments were captured. No one thought to station provost guards to direct the men to the safety of Cemetery Hill; instead, they roamed around until they were captured. At several places, however, including the town square, artillery was positioned that cleared the streets of approaching Southern soldiers. But it was too little, too late, as thousands were hustled away as prisoners.

As the Federal troops began their retreat, John Burns discarded his rifle and buried his ammunition. Wounded three times and captured by the on-rushing Southerners, he professed to be merely a bystander caught in the fighting. His captors placed him into a wagon and returned him to his home. Burns received lasting fame for his role in the Battle of Gettysburg.

The contest for the ridges west and north of Gettysburg lasted from 10:00 A.M. to well past 4:00 P.M., with but a single midday lull. Thirteen Union brigades with 22,000 men fought seventeen Confederate brigades at a strength of about 27,000. Aggregate losses were close to 17,000; 10,000 Union and 7,000 Confederate, and losses exceeding 50 percent were not uncommon. On the Union side, approximately the same number of men were captured (5,000) as were killed or wounded.

In numbers and proportions, the I Corps' losses exceeded those of the XI Corps by 50 percent. The I Corps carried 1,000 more men on its rolls than the XI Corps, and two-thirds of its 6,000 losses (almost 60 percent) were killed or wounded. The XI Corps lost 3,800 men, half of whom were listed as captured or missing.

Reynolds's loss was a great blow to the Union. The Union could ill afford to lose one of the Army of the Potomac's most competent and popular generals. Knowing that only a third of his corps had arrived and that he was up against a large enemy force, Reynolds fearlessly rode to the head of his troops to calm them before sending them into battle. In the end, he lived up to his philosophy that "volunteer troops were better led than driven."

CEMETERY HILL
4:00 TO 6:00 P.M, JULY 1

As the Confederates moved through the town, they could see the enemy taking positions on Cemetery Hill. Within a short time, almost forty cannon overlooked the town and surrounding areas. To the southeast was another large eminence called Culp's Hill. This strategic hill apparently was unoccupied. There were more than four hours of daylight left and *Early's* division was still fairly fresh. Standing on Seminary Ridge, *Lee* scanned the hills with his binoculars. He could see the apparently disorganized Union troops disappearing to the east and over the crest of the ridge a mile from where he stood. Behind them he could see *Ewell's* corps driving the stragglers through town. Lee concluded that an immediate drive by *Ewell* could shove the teetering Federals off Cemetery Hill and end the day with a decisive Confederate victory. A courier was soon galloping toward *Ewell's* headquarters with an important message from Lee.

Suffering from the heat, fatigue, and the pain of his infected stump of a leg, *Ewell* only wanted to rest himself and his men. *Lee's* order was "to attack that hill, if practicable, but to avoid a general engagement until the arrival of other divisions of the army." *Ewell* reasoned that his troops were in no shape to continue. They were tired from the march to the battlefield and from the bitter fighting that had left them in control of the field. Additionally, the town's confusing streets, which had hindered the Union soldiers, had also wreaked havoc on his brigades' formations. To complicate matters, rumors kept surfacing about fresh Union troops marching on their left flank and rear, convincing *Ewell* to dispatch fresh troops to guard against any such movement.

Despite the urging of several subordinates, who with *Lee* could see the tactical importance of Cemetery and Culp's Hills, *Ewell* decided to wait until *Major General Edward Johnson's* division arrived. *Gordon*, whose men had knocked the XI Corps back to the town earlier in the day, actually ordered his men to take the heights. But repeated orders finally forced him to pull back. So distraught were some of *Ewell's* officers that they stomped off in anger. *Major General Isaac Trimble*, a crusty old fighter who was serving as a volunteer aide, turned to *Ewell* and said, "General, give me a division and I will take that hill." When *Ewell* declined, *Trimble* asked for a brigade and then a regiment. When those requests were denied, he threw his sword at *Ewell's* feet and stormed away, muttering that he could no longer serve under such an officer. *Lee* eventually rode over to *Ewell's* headquarters to directly order him to take the heights. A scouting party had found Culp's Hill unoccupied and *Ewell* agreed to take it as soon as *Johnson's* division arrived, which was expected momentarily.

Unlike *Lee*, who had arrived on the field in the afternoon, Meade elected to remain at his temporary headquarters in Taneytown, Maryland, thirteen miles south of Gettysburg. This put him at the center of the army's operations—a good place for a commanding general who had not yet decided where the major battle would be fought. During the day, he anxiously awaited developments before deciding the final disposition of his troops. Meade most trusted Reynolds and Major General Winfield Hancock, and they were his eyes and ears on the first day of battle. The messages transmitted on the morning of July 1 by Buford and Reynolds had been incomplete, so by early afternoon Meade felt he needed a more accurate picture of what was transpiring. Since Reynolds was now dead, Meade asked Hancock to ride to the battlefield, with broad authority to continue the fight at Gettysburg or to pull the troops back to the preselected position on Big Pipe Creek in Maryland. During the first two or three miles of the journey, Hancock rode in an ambulance, carefully studying maps of the area. Once familiarized, he quickly mounted his horse and rode to Gettysburg. Meade knew that because Howard outranked Hancock, a disagreement might arise when they met, but he reasoned that this was a unique situation. There are several versions of what happened when Hancock arrived on Cemetery Hill and saluted Howard, between 3:30 and 4:00 P.M. According to one account, Hancock and Howard struck an agreement—Meade's orders to Hancock were to determine if the Gettysburg area was suited to a general engagement. If Howard agreed with Hancock's assessment, the decision would be made. Hancock liked the looks of the ground around Gettysburg and (fortunately) Howard agreed, sealing the fate of the Confederacy. Another plausible story is that they agreed to split command of the field. Either way, Hancock believed that Gettysburg was a good place to stop *Lee's* invasion, a view he communicated to Meade.

Hancock ordered the men to continue fortifying Cemetery Hill. More than forty cannon from the I and XI Corps were then in the cemetery, wreaking havoc on the headstones and vegetation. Hancock soon brought some order to the Union position. With his handsome appearance, military bearing, and calm, soldierly crispness, Hancock generated confidence in men and officers alike. A kind of electricity buzzed in the area as he inspected the positions. Observing that Culp's Hill was unoccupied, Hancock sent the Iron Brigade to its western slope; the 7th Indiana formed on its right. The wisdom of this precaution became apparent before the sun went down.

JOHNSON ATTEMPTS TO TAKE CULP'S HILL

Johnson's division arrived in Gettysburg via Chambersburg Pike about dusk, having marched twenty-five miles that day. *Ewell* told him to take Culp's Hill if a reconnaissance showed it to be unoccupied. After sending a party forward, *Johnson* moved his brigades through the town to an attack position on Benner's Hill. It was just at this time that the 7th Indiana (Wadsworth's division), which had been guarding supplies on Emmitsburg Road, and therefore was fresh, arrived on Culp's Hill. The Hoosiers bagged some of *Johnson's* scouts and fired on the rest. Those not captured ran back to tell *Johnson* that the hill was indeed occupied. Rather than risking an evening attack against an enemy of unknown strength, *Johnson* decided to wait until morning, when he could better size up the situation. Assuming that *Johnson* was about to attack the hill, *Ewell* turned in for the night. It was only later that he learned that the attack had been delayed. When he did, he ordered *Johnson* to prepare to take the hill in the morning.

THE SITUATION AT THE END OF THE FIRST DAY

At about 7:00 P.M., Hancock sent a report to Meade recommending that the battle be fought at Gettysburg. Then, at about sunset, Hancock turned command of the field over to newly arrived Major General Henry Slocum, who outranked Howard, and rode back to Taneytown to meet with Meade. He also resumed command of the II Corps. Meade readily accepted Hancock's recommendation and ordered the remainder of his army to immediately march on Gettysburg. While he discarded the notion of fighting along Big Pipe Creek, he still had not decided whether to assume the offensive or defensive when the armies met again the next day.

Meade left Taneytown at about 10:00 P.M. and arrived about midnight. Before his arrival, six or seven Union generals met at the gatehouse of Evergreen Cemetery. In the shadowy room illuminated by a single candle, they agreed that this was a good place to fight it out with *Lee*. When they expressed their feelings about the position to Meade, he remarked, "I am glad to hear you say so, gentlemen, for it is too late to leave it." The remainder of the night was spent inspecting and adjusting the positions on Cemetery Hill and Culp's Hill. General Meade extended his line to the left (south) toward two hills, the Round Tops, posted artillery, and perfected dispositions of fresh troops that would soon arrive. Slocum's XII Corps had arrived at about 5:00 P.M., Hancock's II Corps arrived between 5:30 and 6:30, and Major General Daniel Sickles's III Corps arrived around dusk. Major General George Sykes's V Corps arrived early on July 2 (See Map 5, p. 66).

After completing the inspection with his generals, Meade decided to go on the offensive as soon as Major General John Sedgwick's VI Corps arrived the next day. With about 15,000 men, it was the largest corps in the Army of the Potomac. During the evening of July 1, Sedgewick and his men camped near Manchester, Maryland, about thirty-five miles from Gettysburg. This position, between York and Baltimore, was a perfect one if *Lee* reversed his advance and struck south. After receiving urgent orders to come to the battlefield, the corps arrived between 2:00 and 3:00 P.M. July 2 in a march that has few rivals in American history. The corps formed a vital reserve and arrived just as *Lee* unleashed his savage attacks against Meade's positions.

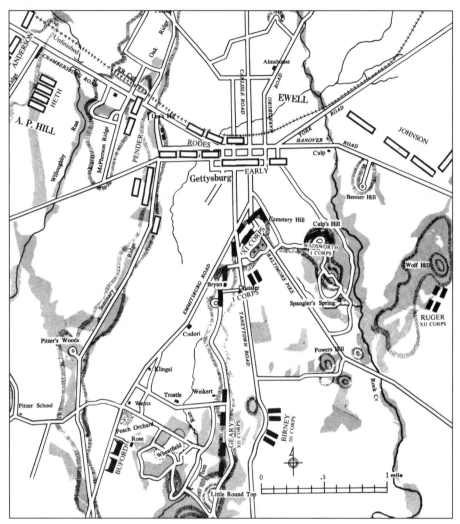

Map 5. The situation at sundown, July 1.

Meade was not the only one who did not sleep that night. The men needed little urging to fortify their positions by every possible means, though this was in no way common even at this point in the war. The apprehensive families who remained in their farmhouses could hear the tramp of marching feet as arriving units were directed into their assigned sectors, the neighing of horses, the rumbling of artillery and creaking of straining harnesses, and the barking of commands.

The Confederates were mostly inactive during this time, but the sounds of axes chopping down trees and picks making trenches on Cemetery and Culp's Hills caused dread in many of the men. They knew that they would be testing those defenses the next day.

Thanks to Confederate congestion on the main road from Chambersburg to Gettysburg, *Lee's* vague orders to *Ewell* on the afternoon of July 1, the absence of *Stuart's* cavalry, and more rapid marching, the Army of the Potomac barely won the race to assemble at Gettysburg with the most men. By daylight July 2, Meade's entire army was present, with the exception of the VI Corps and the cavalry divisions of Brigadier Generals David Gregg and Judson Kilpatrick, all of which reached the field by late afternoon of the second day.

Daylight similarly found *Lee's* army fully assembled except for *Brigadier General Evander Law's* brigade of *Hood's* division, *Major General George Pickett's* division, and *Stuart's* cavalry, which showed up in the late afternoon of July 2, thoroughly jaded after its fruitless ride around the Union army. Consequently, the men in blue held a substantial strength advantage over the Rebels that would be increased by more than 20,000 when the rest of both armies reached the field.

THE SECOND DAY

Dispositions of the Opposing Forces, July 2

At dawn on July 2, the Union position south of town resembled a large fishhook. Culp's Hill formed the right flank of the army and the barb of the hook. The eastern side of the hill was held by Slocum's XII Corps and the remnant of Wadsworth's division (I Corps) held the northern side. Cemetery Hill to the west was occupied by Howard's XI Corps. The shank of the hook extended along Cemetery Ridge south to the Round Tops. The northern part of Cemetery Ridge was occupied by the remainder of the I Corps. On its left, deployed south along the ridge, was Hancock's II Corps. To his left was Sickles's III Corps, whose line did not quite extend to the Round Tops at this time. All of the units on Cemetery Ridge faced Seminary Ridge to the west, where the Confederates were positioned. Thin lines of skirmishers from both armies were thrown out in the contested area between the ridges. When Sykes's V Corps arrived, it was placed in reserve behind the II and III Corps.

The position was more than three miles long, but because of its curve at the northern end and the presence of good roads in its immediate rear, it had what is known as "interior lines." Troops and supplies could be shifted easily from one part of the line to another to meet changing threats. Each end of the Union line rested on or was close to rocky hills that were easily defended. These hills (particularly Cemetery Hill and Little Round Top) also were good observation points, and artillery placed on them could rake the battlefield. Low stone walls dotted the field, providing good protection for the infantry.

Lee's position enveloped the Federals' to the north and west of the hills and ridges. The men of *Hill's* III Corps held the right flank along Seminary Ridge. The line extended to the north, were *Ewell's* line wrapped around Cemetery and Culp's Hills and ended on Benner's Hill. As *Longstreet's* divisions arrived on July 2, they moved south to extend *Lee's* right flank along Seminary Ridge to a position opposite Little Round Top.

The Confederates were in an inferior tactical position, but their successes of July 1 had given them possession of the town and firmly secured their escape routes to the west. The distance between the armies had, in one day, been contracted from miles to a few hundred yards of open fields and scattered farm buildings south and west of the town.

THE MORNING OF JULY 2 PASSES QUIETLY

Longstreet was *Lee's* most respected corps commander. A proponent of active defense, in which the enemy is lured into attacking where you are strong, *Longstreet* tenaciously tried to persuade *Lee* that he should move around the Union left flank rather than continue the offensive at Gettysburg. *Longstreet* argued that such a movement would put the Confederates between Washington and the Union army, forcing Meade to attack. If *Lee* could find a good defensive position, the war would soon be over. *Lee* did not ignore his lieutenant's advice but decided it was flawed. Given the army's large wagon train, it was not nearly as mobile as *Longstreet* seemed to think. Also, to disengage invited an attack when the Army of Northern Virginia was most vulnerable.

This left *Lee* with two options: attack or return to Virginia. Doing nothing was not an option when facing a numerically superior foe because that jeopardized *Lee's* long line of communication with Virginia. No, he had brought his army into Pennsylvania to force a showdown that would lead to a negotiated peace. *Lee* simply told *Longstreet*, "If Meade is there tomorrow, I will attack him."

Part of *Lee's* predicament was that he did not expect to find the Union army in front of him. His usually dependable cavalry commander, *Stuart*, was nowhere to be found and *Lee* did not effectively use the two cavalry brigades at his disposal to scout the Union troop dispositions, so his army was operating blindly.

During the night of July 1, *Lee* had considered moving *Early's* division to the opposite end of his line and taking the Round Tops, which sat unoccupied on the vulnerable Union left flank. *Early* vigorously disagreed, saying that the march would be too long and time-consuming. It would also hurt morale, he reasoned, as it meant leaving ground his troops had fought so hard to capture. If the move had been made that evening, however, the outcome of the battle may have been quite different, as Little Round Top would have been in Confederate hands on July 2.

Following separate conferences with *Ewell* and *Longstreet* during the morning of July 2, *Lee* finally formulated his plan for the day. Never did he assemble his three corps commanders during the battle to discuss strategy or coordinate planning. Instead, he spoke to each individually, which resulted in confusion, a weakened overall plan, and almost a total lack of cooperation. Meade fought the battle quite differently, calling several meetings with all of his corps commanders to discuss tactics and ensure cooperation when it was needed. This was a major reason for Meade's success at Gettysburg.

It is clear that *Lee* was "not himself" during the battle; some have attributed it to ill health. He was seen running to the rear several times during the battle, probably suffering from diarrhea. Fresh fruit was abundant along the march route and many men experienced stomach distress during the campaign. He may have also experienced a heart attack sometime during this period of the war.

According to *Lee's* plan for July 2, *Longstreet's* two newly arriving divisions were to circle around to the south, then attack diagonally in a northeastern direction along Emmitsburg Road to roll up Meade's left flank. Without *Stuart's* cavalry, *Lee* erroneously thought the flank was along Emmitsburg Road, at the Peach Orchard. The III Corps actually occupied Cemetery Ridge. *Ewell* was to attack simultaneously from the north and drive the Federals from Culp's and Cemetery Hills. *Hill's* two divisions that had been weakened by the fighting on July 1 were to hold the Union troops in the center of the line by feigning an attack; a fresh division under *Major General Richard Anderson* was to storm Cemetery Ridge. *Ewell* was told to attack when he heard *Longstreet's* guns open, presumably at 11:00 A.M.

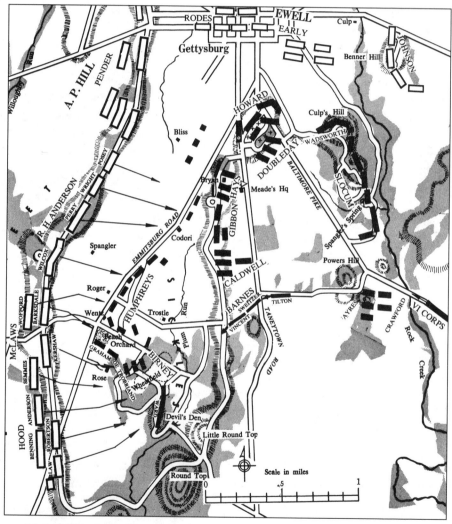

Map 6. The start of Longstreet's *attack, July 2.*

It was a good plan, with one problem. *Lee* was unaware of the exact locations of the Union troops—a fatal error when making plans to defeat an enemy. Though he knew that some reinforcements had arrived, without his cavalry, he did not know the exact numbers or dispositions of the enemy. Losing his patience, *Lee* ordered horsemen to disperse in all directions to find his wayward cavalry commander during the night of July 1.

Lee probably would have liked to attack as early on July 2 as possible, since every hour of delay gave the Federals time to strengthen their positions. But *Longstreet's* men were not in position, so with the exception of occasional artillery fire and skirmishing between pickets, there was no serious fighting on the morning of July 2. Except for *Lee*, no one seemed eager to resume the attack. The morning respite was welcomed after the long marches the men had endured during the campaign and the hard battle they had fought the day before.

After allowing *Johnson's* division to pass on July 1, *Longstreet's* two divisions marched rapidly to Gettysburg, arriving soon after sunrise on July 2. His third division, under *Pickett*, was left at Chambersburg to guard wagon trains, a job more suitable for the missing cavalry. In addition to being unhappy with *Lee's* battle plans, *Longstreet* was upset with his orders to attack with only two divisions. Several times he asked Lee for permission to wait until *Pickett's* division arrived, explaining that he felt like he was going into battle with "one boot off."

Lee declined his subordinate's request but did let *Longstreet* wait until *Law's* brigade arrived. The unit had left New Guilford at 3:00 A.M. and marched twenty-four miles in nine hours without a break, arriving on the battlefield just before noon.

Besides not having *Longstreet's* troops in position, *Lee* could not attack in the early morning because a party he had sent out to scout the Union left flank had not returned. The men later confirmed that the Union line stretched far to the south, but they could not determine with any certainty whether the Round Tops were occupied. The reconnaissance effort was so poor that one had to wonder if the men were riding about blindfolded.

With this information, *Lee* was forced to modify his plan (See Map 7). The attack would be made *en echelon*, starting with *Longstreet's* rightmost brigade. After it became fully engaged, the one on its left would attack, then the one on its left, and so on. Like a row of falling dominoes, the attacks would be launched until *Longstreet's* and *Hill's* divisions were thrown into battle. Any Federal troops pulled away from the front to meet the attack at another location would leave a soft spot that would be exploited by the newly advancing troops. Ultimately, the tactic could have discouraged any attempt to reinforce parts of the line being charged. *Ewell's* orders remained the same—strike the Union right when he heard *Longstreet's* guns.

About noon, *Longstreet* set his men in motion to the jumping-off points on Warfield Ridge and the southern end of Seminary Ridge. He believed that stealth was more important than speed, and one historian has called this episode "as strange a march as was ever made on an American battlefield." *Longstreet's* two divisions first moved away from the battlefield (the way they had come) on Chambersburg Pike for about three miles, then turned onto a road leading south. Inexplicably, *Longstreet's* troops were led by the *Lee* aide who had conducted the early morning reconnaissance. The officer had never been on this field before, and even he could not believe that he had been ordered to find a route for *Longstreet's* men. After an hour, *Longstreet* realized that the enemy would see his column as it crossed Herr Ridge. Halting his men, he ordered them to turn around and retrace their steps. Finally, the column stopped within a half-mile of Chambersburg Pike and marched south along the west bank of Willoughby Run to its assigned position. Little did *Longstreet* know that his efforts were useless—Federal signal men on Little Round Top had observed the movement. *Colonel E. Porter Alexander*, commanding *Longstreet's* artillery corps, did not retrace his steps, but simply continued to the south and swung in a wide arc to the east, arriving in position several hours before the infantry. The effect of *Longstreet's* delay in reaching his assigned position has been hotly debated ever since the battle.

By the time *Longstreet's* divisions reached their destination, they had marched between eight and thirteen miles through blazing heat. Still full of fight, they were ready to end the war by catching the enemy on the flank and rolling it up, as *Stonewall Jackson* had done just weeks before at Chancellorsville.

SICKLES UNCOVERS THE ROUND TOPS
3:00 P.M., JULY 2

Over on Cemetery Ridge, the Union high command was busily preparing for the expected attack. When Slocum's XII Corps arrived on the battlefield the day before, Brigadier General Alpheus Williams's division was ordered to take position on Culp's Hill. Brigadier General John Geary's division was to occupy the southern part of Cemetery Ridge and Little Round Top until relieved by Sickles's III Corps. Geary grew impatient when Sickles did not show. Believing he could wait no longer to join his own corps on Culp's Hill, Geary marched his division away, leaving the vital Round Tops unoccupied, except for the signal corps.

Sickles did not care for his assigned position on the left flank. He considered it to be weak, especially since his artillery was masked by woods. Instead, he liked the high ground along Emmitsburg Road in front of his position, a half-mile farther west, and thought it should be seized before the Confederates could take possession. As Sickles extended his line to the south along Cemetery Ridge, as ordered, he found that he was no longer on an elevation, but instead was in a marshy depression between the ridge and Little Round Top. Uncertain about what to do, he requested advice from Meade between 6:00 and 7:00 A.M., who responded that he should occupy Geary's prior position.

Sickles fretted all morning that the Confederates would capture the high ground along Emmitsburg Road. Only weeks before at Chancellorsville, his corps had been crushed after the Confederates took the high ground in front of him; he was determined that it would not happen again. Unwilling to wait any longer, Sickles rode over to Meade's headquarters, seeking permission to occupy the advanced position. Preoccupied with an expected attack by *Ewell* on his right, Meade had paid little attention to his left flank and was unprepared to act on Sickles's request. Instead, he sent his chief of artillery, Brigadier General Henry Hunt, to examine the terrain and report back. Hunt agreed with Sickles about some of the advantages of the more advanced position, but pointed out a number of serious deficiencies. Sickles's desired position was to be 1½ miles long, double that of his current line, and if the move was made, his right flank would no longer connect with the left of Hancock's II Corps. The gap could be filled by bringing up Sykes's V Corps from its reserve position, but that decision was Meade's.

During the early afternoon, the Federal signal station on Little Round Top reported Confederate columns on the move in the woods along Herr Ridge. Seeing no enemy in his front, Sickles threw out Berdan's Sharpshooters and the 3d Maine. They cautiously crossed the open fields and encountered enemy skirmishers in Pitzer's Woods on Seminary Ridge. After dispersing them, they came face-to-face with three long lines of infantry from *Brigadier General Cadmus Wilcox's* brigade of *Major General Richard Anderson's* division (*Hill's* corps). For twenty-five minutes, these two small Federal units battled the Rebel brigade until being forced to withdraw.

Sickles now realized that Confederate infantry was massing in his front and he could wait no longer. At 3:00, with colors flying, 10,000 men in several battle lines swept down the gentle slope of Cemetery Ridge and crossed the valley to take the heights along Emmitsburg Road. Unfortunately, the movement placed the III Corps about a half-mile in front of the rest of the army, with both of its flanks "in the air." To make matters worse, Brigadier General Andrew Humphreys's division was north of the Wentz farm along Emmitsburg Road, facing northwest, while Major General David Birney's division faced west, creating a sharp angle at the Wentz house and the adjacent Peach Orchard.

At midafternoon, Meade called a conference of his corps commanders. Sickles sent a request to be excused because he was in direct contact with the enemy and expected an attack momentarily. The request was denied.

The Leister House. General Meade's headquarters during the battle, it was the scene of several counsels of war. The house was evacuated during the afternoon of July 3 because of the intense Confederate artillery barrage launched against this area prior to the Pickett-Pettigrew-Trimble charge.

As Sickles arrived at Meade's headquarters at the small Leister house, rifle and artillery fire broke out from his corps' position. Meade immediately dismissed the generals and met Sickles at the door. Both generals then galloped off toward the Peach Orchard.

Possibly realizing his error for the first time, Sickles offered to return his troops to their former position on Cemetery Ridge. "Too late," Meade answered curtly. "You must fight it out where you are; I'll move troops at once to support you." The shells and bullets whizzing through the air disturbed Old Baldy, Meade's horse, which usually took such situations in stride. The animal reared and galloped off, with Meade pulling ineffectually at the reins. The conversation with Sickles was abruptly terminated as Meade was carried at a fast gait to his headquarters. Finally gaining control of his horse, he issued orders to meet the crisis. Part of Sykes's reserve was hurried up to fill

Modern view of the Leister House. Large trees now obscure the view. To the left of the house, just out of view is the Cyclorama. Plans are being made to remove it and the visitor center and restore the area to its original appearance. You will pass this area between Tour Stops 12 and 13.

the Sickles-created gap on Cemetery Ridge; other units were alerted to be ready to move quickly. Meade displayed decisive generalship at this stage of the battle, taking a risk that could have proven disastrous. By shifting troops from other sectors of the battlefield, particularly the right on Culp's Hill, Meade bet that he would not be attacked there and, if he was, that the remaining men could hold the line.

LONGSTREET AT LAST ATTACKS
4:00 P.M., July 2

Longstreet's divisions were finally in position by 4 P.M., many hours later than *Lee* had wished. They quickly realized that the Round Tops were unoccupied. Both *Hood* and one of his brigade commanders, *Brigadier General Evander Law*, ordered scouts to find the enemy's left flank. Both groups returned, unmolested by a single Union soldier. There were thousands of Federals on the ridge to the north, but incredibly, none occupied the Round Tops. They also observed a large and carelessly guarded wagon train and an artillery reserve on the eastern side of the Round Tops. In *Hood's* opinion, a radical change of plan was in order. He sent the information to *Longstreet* and asked to move farther south, circle around the Round Tops, outflank the Union position, then drive north, taking Little Round Top. *Longstreet's* response was curt: "Attack as ordered."

Hood was perhaps the most aggressive division commander in *Lee's* army, so his hesitation to attack as ordered was not construed as a reluctance to engage the enemy. After several rejections of his written requests, he rode over to *Longstreet* and literally pleaded for permission to modify the attack plan. To attack along Emmitsburg Road would invite deadly fire from his front and flank, and the irregular ground and fields with boulders would create havoc with his attack formations. *Longstreet* again rejected the request because it would further delay the attack, which should have been launched in the morning. Although he pressed the issue, *Hood* was finally and forcefully told that *Lee* had ordered him to attack along Emmitsburg Road, and he would carry out those orders. Realizing that he was wasting his time, *Hood* returned to his division and prepared for an attack he knew would create many widows and orphans in both North and South.

The attack on the Union left began when sixty Confederate guns opened fire on Sickles's line. *Longstreet's* infantry was poised to open the *en echelon* attack. As each brigade moved forward, the brigade on its left was to take up the advance until all three divisions—*Hood's, McLaws's*, and

Anderson's—entered action. As a result, the fighting was fragmented and less effective than a coordinated assault would have been by the four divisions on a narrower front.

WARREN SAVES LITTLE ROUND TOP
4:00 P.M., JULY 2

While Meade was finally examining the III Corps' exposed position, he ordered his chief engineer, Brigadier General Gouverneur Warren, to take a closer look at Little Round Top, from whose direction rifle fire could be heard. To his dismay, he found the hill unoccupied except for a handful of Union signalmen, who were packing up to leave.

Warren's background as a West Point-trained engineer helped him realize how important these heights were to both armies. Suspecting enemy infantry in the woods below, he ordered cannon fire into it. As the hidden troops dove for cover, Warren could see the gleam of their bayonets, and he realized that trouble was imminent. Without hesitation, Warren ordered the signalmen to continue waving their flags, giving the enemy the impression that Little Round Top was occupied, then he relayed messages to Meade and Sickles to immediately send troops. Hastening down the hill, he sought out Sykes, whose V Corps he knew to be in the area. Sykes agreed to send a brigade to defend the hill, and soon a messenger was galloping in search of one of his division commanders, Brigadier General James Barnes.

Over on the far right of *Hood's* line, *Colonel William Oates's* 15th Alabama of *Law's* brigade advanced toward the Round Tops. Before the attack, a group of twenty-two water carriers were selected to fill the regiment's canteens, but they had not returned when the order to advance was given. *Oates's* men had to fight a pitched battle in scorching heat after a twenty-four-hour march without water.

While *Law's* other regiments wheeled to the left to hit Birney's division, *Oates* continued straight ahead. With part of the 47th Alabama, *Oates's* men scrambled up the steep side of Round Top. *Oates* liked the position and envisioned what artillery could do from there. His musings were interrupted when a messenger brought orders to descend the hill and capture Little Round Top. As they made their descent, *Oates* saw the wagon train and ordered his men to capture it. Just then a galling fire erupted from the side of Little Round Top where the 20th Maine, under Colonel Joshua Chamberlain, had just taken position.

While *Oates's* men were resting on Round Top, Little Round Top remained undefended. As the messenger for Barnes galloped along Taneytown Road, he was intercepted by Colonel Strong Vincent, whose brigade was resting by the side of the road. Insisting on reading the message, Vincent immediately ordered his brigade to double-quick up the hill, knowing that he was disobeying orders. Up to this point in the war, it had been the Southern officers who showed the most initiative, disobeying orders when conditions warranted. Now a Union commander did the same, with very positive results. Vincent's men took their positions on the hill barely ten minutes before *Oates's* men arrived. The 20th Maine held the leftmost part of the line; Vincent's other three regiments formed to the right of it. Vincent's orders to Chamberlain were straightforward: "This is the left of the Union line. . .You are to hold this ground at all costs."

A volley from the 20th Maine on the hill caused *Oates* to temporarily abandon his attempt to capture the wagons and turn toward capturing Little Round Top. The fighting along the hill was desperate, at times hand-to-hand. Each attack was repulsed with heavy losses on both sides. A third regiment from *Law's* brigade and two from *Robertson's* attacked Vincent's

View From Little Round Top. The elevated region in front of Little Round Top is called Houck's Ridge. The boulders of Devil's Den can be seen to the left of the photograph; in front of it is the Slaughter Pen. On the right, units from General Crawford's Pennsylvania Reserves Division counterattacked and drove back the Confederate infantry during the evening of July 2. The Wheatfield is hidden from view behind the trees.

center and right. After continuous battering, the 16th Michigan on the right of the line gave way. Seeing the danger, Vincent ran forward to encourage his troops, only to go down with a mortal wound. He was later acknowledged by Union and Confederate sources to be the man who saved Little Round Top and the Federal army. For his actions, he was promoted to brigadier general on his deathbed.

Warren was not through with his heroics. Seeing Brigadier General Stephen Weed's brigade of Brigadier General Romeyn Ayer's Division (V Corps) marching toward the Peach Orchard to support Sickles, Warren ordered it to aid Vincent. The first regiment to arrive, the 140th New York under Colonel Patrick O'Rorke, stormed up the hill and fired on the onrushing Confederates when they were within thirty yards of the crest of the hill. The appearance of this Zouave regiment, dressed in baggy blue pants, red jackets, and fezzes, was so startling that several Southerners threw down their arms or retreated. Warren also ordered Lieutenant Charles Hazlett's six-gun battery to take position on the hill. The Confederates were thrown back, but not without heavy losses, including the mortal wounding of Weed, Hazlett, and O'Rorke. The last's men were so enraged that their commander had been hit that they pumped seventeen bullets into the Southerner who mortally wounded him. Over on Vincent's left flank, *Oates's* men had stormed up the hill five times, and five times they were driven back with heavy losses on both sides. They tried to flank the Union position, but Chamberlain stretched his line and bent it backward to meet the challenge. By 6:30 P.M., *Oates's* men were exhausted and dehydrated. With his force decimated and sharpshooters threatening his rear, *Oates* was close to defeat. Little did he know that the 20th Maine also was having troubles of its own: it had taken heavy losses and was nearly out of ammunition. But Chamberlain refused to give up the hill, so he ordered his men to fix bayonets and sweep the Alabamans from Little Round Top.

The sight of Chamberlain's men charging down the hill was too much for *Oates's* men. They fled down the hill and back up Round Top. Going into the battle with 500 men, the 15th Alabama came out with only 223. The 20th Maine fared a little better. Out of 386 men, it lost about 190. Finally realizing the importance of Round Top, Colonel Joseph Fisher's Pennsylvania brigade (Brigadier General Samuel Crawford's division, V Corps), along with the 20th Maine, moved up and occupied the hill that evening.

The conventional wisdom is that for an attack against heights to succeed, attackers should outnumber defenders by at least three to one. During the initial attacks, 2,016 men in five Confederate regiments attacked 1,336 Federals in four regiments. Such an attack was futile, and when O'Rorke's 450 men were added to the equation, the South had virtually no chance to take the hill. This futility was repeated throughout the afternoon. Rather than concentrating their efforts in one area, the Southern leaders dissipated their strength trying to take multiple objectives.

DEVIL'S DEN
4:30 P.M., JULY 2

Sickles's flawed deployment of Birney's division on his corps' left soon became evident. Composed of three brigades, the division was ordered to defend a three-quarter-mile stretch from Devil's Den on the south to the Peach Orchard to the north. Brigadier General Hobart Ward's brigade was assigned the woods on Houck's Ridge, just to the southeast of the Rose farm, as well

The Slaughter Pen. After capturing Devil's Den, Law's brigade swept into this region, where it lost almost 200 men in bitter fighting.

as the boulders of Devil's Den to the south. Brigadier General Charles Graham's brigade was ordered to hold the Peach Orchard salient and Colonel Regis de Trobriand's brigade was assigned the position in between. Because of the length of the line, large gaps existed between each brigade.

Brigadier General Jerome Robertson (*Hood's* division) moved his brigade forward to attack Ward, only to realize that two of his regiments had peeled off and joined in *Law's* attack on Little Round Top. *Robertson's* orders were to take the Rose Woods and Devils Den; he would try to do just that with his remaining two regiments (1st Texas and 3d Arkansas). Outnumbered two-to-one by Ward's troops, these two regiments held their own during intense fighting. Finally, as the 124th New York pushed *Robertson's* regiments back in a wild fight, it in turn was stopped in its tracks by *Brigadier General Henry Benning's* brigade, whose turn it was to enter the fray. *Benning* was to have helped capture Little Round Top, but seeing a

The modern view of the Slaughter Pen looks remarkably like it did in 1863. This site is in front of you as you park at Tour Stop 8A.

sister brigade in trouble, he turned to *Robertson's* sector. After intense fighting, three Federal cannon were captured and their supporting infantry pushed back toward Little Round Top.

While two of *Benning's* regiments joined *Robertson* in throwing Ward out of the Rose Woods, his other regiments were attacking Devil's Den and the Slaughter Pen, just to the south. As these units attacked from the west, two regiments from *Law's* brigade hit the Federal troops from the south. Attacked in front, flank, and rear, the Union troops finally gave way at about 6:00 P.M. The Southerners moved in, planted their flags on the topmost elevation of Devil's Den, and there they remained until the battle ended on July 3. Sharpshooters were positioned at Devil's Den to fire at Union soldiers on Little Round Top, and many officers and men positioned on the hill were picked off in this manner.

WHIRLPOOL AT THE WHEATFIELD
5:45 P.M., JULY 2

During the desperate fighting at Little Round Top, Rose's Woods, Devil's Den, and the Slaughter Pen, *Hood's* last brigade under *Brigadier General George Anderson* moved forward. His objective was the center of Birney's line held by de Trobriand at the Wheatfield. Earlier in the fighting, two of de Trobriand's regiments were rushed to other parts of the field, leaving only three regiments to handle *Anderson's* attack. In response to the dangerous situation, brigades under Colonels Jacob Sweitzer and William Tilton from Barnes's division (V Corps) and two regiments from Humphreys's division were rushed forward to de Trobriand's aid. These troops held favorable ground and repelled the assault. Charge followed countercharge in the turbulent area. Finally, realizing that he was getting nowhere, *Anderson* decided to delay any more attacks until fresh Confederate troops arrived.

Longstreet's second powerful division, under *Major General Lafayette McLaws*, then entered the fray. It had been about ninety minutes since *Hood* began his attack; this delay permitted Meade to shift troops to his beleaguered left flank, with positive results. Why *Longstreet* waited so long to launch *McLaws's* attack has never been adequately answered.

McLaws's first brigade, under *Brigadier General Joseph Kershaw*, came to *Anderson's* aid. Seeing this new threat, Tilton adjusted his brigade's alignment, but in doing so exposed Sweitzer's flank. Their nervous commander, Barnes, pulled both brigades back, leaving only de Trobriand's small band to check the two Confederate brigades.

Attacked in the front and both flanks, de Trobriand reluctantly ordered his men to withdraw across the large Wheatfield. In response to urgent pleas from Birney, Hancock rushed Brigadier General John Caldwell's large division (II Corps) from Cemetery Ridge to help stem the tide, which arrived at about 6:40 P.M. One of Caldwell's brigades was called the Irish Brigade because of its preponderance of soldiers from the Emerald Isle. With the battle swirling around them, their chaplain, Father William Corby, stepped up on a rock to offer absolution. The men were told that a Christian burial would be withheld from any soldier who deserted his flag and did not live up to his responsibility. The sight of an entire brigade on its knees receiving absolution at the height of battle was awe-inspiring.

With Caldwell's appearance, *Kershaw* requested reinforcements. *McLaw's* next brigade, under *Brigadier General Paul Semmes*, ran forward. Caldwell's troops fired into the approaching Southerners, taking out many of the Georgians, including *Semmes*, who was mortally wounded. Within fifteen minutes, Caldwell's division had pushed the Southerners out of the Wheatfield.

Suddenly, the Irish Brigade spied a column moving toward its right flank and rear. The men fervently hoped that it was a wayward regiment from their division. It was not. Another brigade from *McLaw's* division, under *Brigadier General William Wofford,* moved quietly forward toward the Wheatfield and Caldwell's right flank, while *Anderson, Kershaw*, and *Semmes* attacked from other directions. The Irish Brigade and Brigadier General Samuel Zook's brigade were all but surrounded and had to fight their way out to safety. Caldwell's shattered division then retreated to a ridge behind Plum Run.

Sweitzer's brigade then was reinserted into the fray to try to stop the Confederate tide. Attacked on three sides, it was forced to flee under threat of annihilation. One last division stood between the Confederates and Little Round Top/Cemetery Ridge—Ayres's division, made up mostly of U.S. Regulars (V Corps)—and it was sent in. The fighting was short but intense. Ayres's men were almost immediately pushed back; one of his brigades lost almost half its men in a matter of minutes.

An amazing number of regiments from four corps of the two armies were squeezed into the Wheatfield. The fighting was desperate, neither side yielding ground easily until the very earth seemed to ooze blood and the brooks ran in crimson streams. It was aptly termed the "whirlpool" of the battle, because of the way regiment after regiment was seemingly sucked into it for the two and a half hours of fighting.

THE PEACH ORCHARD
6:15 P.M., JULY 2

The men of Graham's brigade (Birney's division) had been worried since taking their advanced position. Only partially closed with a line of thirty artillery pieces supported by infantry, the 500-yard gap between them and de Trobriand's men in the Wheatfield could only bring grief. They watched as the left flank of *Kershaw's* brigade foolishly advanced against these guns and was blown apart, but they knew that it was just a matter of time before the enemy appeared in their front and they would be forced into the battle.

Graham's men had actually not seen much action for the last hour because an intense artillery barrage had forced them to claw the earth for protection. Though not causing much physical damage, the barrage had a tremendous psychological effect. The firing stopped as suddenly as it had started and the men knew what the silence meant. *McLaws's* last brigade, under *Brigadier General William Barksdale,* was advancing against the Union line in perfectly dressed ranks. As it approached, two Pennsylvania regiments (the 57th and 114th) dashed forward to meet them at the Sherfy House. Both paid the price in large numbers of casualties. Graham's men could not withstand this onslaught and fell back to the Peach Orchard, where they tried to regroup and fight again. Union losses were exceptionally heavy during the short fight there. One unit, the 141st Pennsylvania, lost 149 men of the 200 that went into action. Graham went down and was captured. He and almost 1,000 other Federals were scooped up and quickly sent to the rear.

As *Barksdale's* men surged toward the retreating Federals, Confederate artillery moved up to the high ground around the Peach Orchard to fire into the retreating masses. John Wentz, whose house was just across the lane from the Peach Orchard, had remained in his cellar during the battle. When he emerged, he found Confederate guns firing from his front yard. Among the cannoneers was one of Wentz's sons, who had gone South twenty-four years earlier and whom he had not seen since. It was a strange reunion, to say the least.

The Confederates had succeeded so far. Though they had not captured Little Round Top, they had pierced the Union left and center in three places—Devil's Den/Rose Woods, the Wheatfield, and the Peach Orchard. Now it was time to roll up both flanks. About this time, Sickles was struck in the leg by a shell fragment at the Trostle House, near the Peach Orchard and Wheatfield. As he was being carried off on a stretcher, a cigar clamped in his teeth, he continued issuing a stream of orders. (Tour Guide Point 11)

Barksdale's brigade split up. One regiment went straight ahead toward Cemetery Ridge but was met by a hail of canister from artillery massed in its front. *Barksdale's* other three regiments swung to the left and moved northward along Emmitsburg Road to take on the flank of Sickles's other division under Humphreys.

ANDERSON ATTACKS THE UNION CENTER
6:30 P.M., JULY 2

To this point, only Birney's division of the III Corps, along with units of the II and V Corps, had battled the Confederates. As the fighting moved farther north, Humphreys was sucked into the fight. Upon taking command of the III Corps, Birney ordered Humphreys to bend his left flank back to face *Barksdale's* threat. *Barksdale's* three regiments then hit this flank.

Birney could also see two fresh brigades from *Anderson's* division (*Hill's* III Corps) advancing against Humphreys's front and knew that the situation was hopeless. Everyone was ordered to pull back to Cemetery Ridge. No retreat is ever easy, but it is even more difficult while under attack.

While *Barksdale* hit Humphreys's flank, *Wilcox's* and *Perry's* brigades hit them head on and drove the Union division toward the base of Cemetery Ridge with heavy losses. Realizing the seriousness of the situation, Meade asked Hancock to take command of the III Corps and to send a brigade from his own II Corps to help stop *Anderson.* Collecting Colonel George Willard's brigade (Brigadier General Alexander Hays's division), Hancock rode with it toward the growing Confederate threat at the center of the Union line. These men had recently returned to the army after surrendering to Confederate troops the year before at Harper's Ferry. With the reputation as cowards hanging over their heads, they were in an aggressive mood. Quickly formed into line of battle, they barreled into *Barksdale's*

The Trostle Farm. Bigelow's battery made a gallant stand against Barksdale's Mississippians here on the early evening of July 2. Brigadier General Daniel Sickles, the III Corps commander, was struck in the leg by a shell while standing in the farmyard. The limb was later amputated and put on display.

advancing troops. *Barksdale's* men had sustained many casualties up to this point, including their commanding officer. They saw no support behind them and a strong Union force in front of them, so they pulled back.

To *Barksdale's* left, *Wilcox's* and *Perry's* troops stopped as they approached the base of Cemetery Ridge to reform their disorganized ranks before claiming the position. There were few fresh troops in front of *Wilcox*, so taking the ridge would be fairly easy. Seeing this new threat, Hancock found the 1st Minnesota nearby. Although only 262 men strong, the 1st had seen its share of heavy fighting during the war. Unfortunately, Hancock's interaction with the 1st during the march to Gettysburg had not been cordial. Seeing the men cross a stream by walking single file along a fallen log,

Modern view of the Trostle farm. You can still see the hole in the brick-work below the two "diamonds" made by a Confederate cannon ball. This peaceful setting can be seen as you approach Tour Stop 11.

thereby holding up the column, Hancock had its commander, Colonel William Colville, arrested. Now, Hancock freed Colville, and ordered the small regiment to counterattack quickly. Outnumbered four-to-one, the soldiers threw themselves at *Wilcox's* men, who were again moving toward Cemetery Ridge. Despite being on the verge of annihilation, the Minnesotans held their ground until several regiments rushed to their aid. Realizing that the Union position in his front was being strengthened and, like *Barksdale's* men, seeing no support from fresh troops, *Wilcox* decided to withdraw. The losses in the 1st Minnesota were staggering. In less than fifteen minutes of fighting, it lost 82 percent of its men. The gallant unit was never the same and was disbanded the following year.

The other brigade, *Perry's,* also stopped just before reaching Cemetery Ridge. Seeing infantry appear on its flank and receiving musket fire from its front, the brigade commander ordered his men to join *Wilcox's* withdrawal to Seminary Ridge. *Anderson's* third brigade, under *Brigadier General Ambrose Wright,* advanced to *Perry's* left, against Cemetery Ridge. Incredibly, its two right regiments found a gap in the Union line and drove to the crest of the ridge. This was a critical time for the Confederacy. *Wright* realized that he could roll up the Union line by driving to his right or left. But too few of his men remained to exploit the breach. *Wilcox's* and *Perry's* brigades were already back on Seminary Ridge and, to *Wright's* great anger, the two remaining brigades of *Anderson's* division (under *Brigadier Generals Carnot Posey* and *William Mahone*) never advanced to support him. Because these troops did not advance under the *en echelon* tactic, *Pender's* division on *Anderson's* left never entered the fight on the second day.

The Philadelphia Brigade of Brigadier General John Gibbon's division (II Corps) then drove against *Wright's* front while other units hit his flank. Almost surrounded, *Wright* reluctantly ordered a retreat, which could only be undertaken by cutting his way through to safety. Almost half of his brigade was sacrificed on the fields around Cemetery Ridge.

While *Anderson's* division was being repulsed before Cemetery Ridge, the victorious brigades under *Kershaw, Semmes,* and *Anderson* continued their advance toward Little Round Top, just to the south. As they moved through the Plum Run Valley, they were attacked by Colonel William McCandless's brigade of Brigadier General Samuel Crawford's division (V Corps), and pushed back through the Wheatfield. At the same time, Brigadier General Frank Wheaton's brigade of the newly arriving VI Corps pitched into *Wofford's* brigade, which was advancing to the north, driving it back in disorder. The fighting was intense, causing the area to be labeled the Valley of Death.

This ended *Longstreet's* offensive on July 2. During this phase of the battle, eleven brigades from three Confederate divisions engaged twenty-two Federal brigades from the II, III, V, and VI Corps. Thirteen Federal brigades were so badly mauled that they had fully lost their effectiveness. The Southern brigades were not much better off. *Longstreet* later called it "the best three hours of fighting by any troops on any battlefield." The casualties on both sides were staggering. The Southerners lost about 6,000 men; the North, about 9,000.

What *Ewell* and *Hill* were doing during this phase of the battle is a mystery. *Lee* had ordered an *en echelon* attack involving *Longstreet's* and *Hill's* corps on his right and center. *Ewell's* corps was to advance against Culp's Hill as soon as he heard *Longstreet's* guns. *Lee* realized that Meade would rush units from all over the field to beat back attacks on one of his flanks, so it was imperative to engage both simultaneously.

It does not appear that *Ewell* or *Hill* made much effort to comply with *Lee's* orders, nor did *Lee* seem to enforce them. Without pressure on his right flank, Meade was able to strip most of his fresh troops from Culp's Hill with impunity. If *Ewell* had made even a small effort in the afternoon, it would have frozen the Union troops there, and the battle on the opposite flank may have turned out quite differently for the Confederacy. When *Ewell* finally did attack, it was too late.

EARLY TAKES CEMETERY HILL
7:00 P.M., JULY 2

As *Hood's*, *McLaws's*, and *Anderson's* divisions sputtered to a halt at dusk, *Ewell* belatedly awoke to his responsibility. *Rodes's* and *Early's* divisions were ordered to storm Cemetery Hill, while *Johnson's* was to take Culp's Hill (See Map 7, p. 94). Shortly after *Longstreet's* assault had gotten underway, *Ewell's* guns opened on Cemetery and Culp's Hills, but the response from Hunt's massed Union batteries was so destructive that *Ewell* hesitated to attack.

Time ticked away, permitting Meade to move all but one brigade of the XII Corps from Culp's Hill to face *Longstreet's* threat. At about 7:00 P.M., fully two and one-half hours after *Longstreet* engaged the Union left, *Ewell* finally attacked the opposite end of the Union line.

Colonel Leopold von Gilsa's brigade (Barlow's division) of the ill-fated XI Corps that had been routed the day before, was one of the units entrusted with holding the northeastern slope of Cemetery Hill. At sunset, *Early* formed *Hays's* and *Hoke's* brigades for the attack, and a third brigade moved up in support. Charging up the hill, they were hit almost immediately by fire from twenty-two cannon on the heights. Undeterred, they drove forward for 700 yards toward the Northern infantry and eventually crashed through the first line on East Cemetery Hill.

This was but a weakly held line. The Southerners stopped to reform their ranks and charged toward the main Federal line at 8:20 P.M. In the

Cemetery Hill. Driving up the hill, two brigades of Early's division captured Cemetery Hill during the evening of July 2. Their stay was short-lived, however, as Union reinforcements converged on all sides, throwing the Confederates back off the hill.

growing darkness, von Gilsa watched a line of infantry moving toward his position, but thinking they were Union infantry that had been in his front, ordered his men to hold their fire. Despite the pleading of some officers, von Gilsa would not give the order to fire. Finally, with the Confederate line almost on top of his men, the commander of the 153d Pennsylvania countermanded his superior officer's order and screamed for his men to open fire. It was too late. After some hand-to-hand fighting, the Federal troops fled, as they had at Chancellorsville and the day before. It took *Early's* troops an hour to reach the foot of Cemetery Hill, but once they arrived, they routed von Gilsa's troops in a matter of minutes.

Other Union units were flanked and they, too, fled for the rear. The XI Corps commander, Oliver Howard, was almost overrun but quickly rushed nearby regiments into the breach. *Early's* men turned their attention to the batteries on the hill and the fighting turned hand-to-hand as the cannoneers used swabs, spikes, and discarded muskets to defend their precious guns. Despite their efforts, two batteries were captured. With the disintegration of Howard's defensive line, the Confederates occupied the critical summit of Cemetery Hill. Behind them was Baltimore Pike and the rear of the entire Union line.

Modern view of Cemetery Hill looking northeast. Because of the growth of foliage, the site looks quite different than it did in 1863. Monuments commemorating the XI Corps are plentiful on the hill, but no Southern memorials have been erected.

The Confederates did not have long to savor their victory, for they were hit on three sides by a Union counterattack. The night was so dark that the approaching troops, including Colonel Samuel Carroll's brigade (*Hays's* division) of the II Corps, were guided only by musket flashes. Crouching behind a stone wall, the remnants of the two Southern brigades fought valiantly against the counterattacks while casting an eye for aid from their rear. *Hays* saw a line of men coming from the direction of *Rodes's* division and ordered his men not to fire on it. His mistake, the same as von Gilsa's not 30 minutes earlier, helped this Federal force drive *Hays's* men off the hill. The hoped-for aid never arrived, though several brigades were in the vicinity. *Early* himself observed the situation but failed to send forward his reserve brigade, later stating that to have done so would have only led to "useless sacrifice." There was sacrifice, but it was by the two brigades that had gallantly attacked Cemetery Hill without adequate support.

Early was not alone in mismanaging his attack. Units of *Rodes's* division on *Early's* right flank were to have attacked the hill at the same time. But *Rodes* misjudged how long it would take to move his troops through the streets of Gettysburg and, by the time they were in position, *Early's* attack had been repulsed. Seeing the hill bristling with cannon and heavily defended by infantry behind breastworks, *Rodes's* brigade commanders decided to abort the attack.

JOHNSON PARTIALLY SUCCEEDS IN TAKING CULP'S HILL
7:00 P.M., JULY 2

As the battle was developing on Cemetery Hill, *Johnson's* division on the extreme Confederate left flank worked its way slowly toward Culp's Hill. Before the attack, *Johnson's* exposed guns on Benner's Hill dueled with Union artillery on Culp's Hill. Its more advantageous position allowed the Federal artillery finally to force the Confederate pieces from the field, leaving only one battery to cover *Johnson's* infantry when the advance was finally ordered at about 7:00 P.M.

Earlier in the day, Culp's Hill had been strongly held by Wadsworth's depleted division (I Corps) and Slocum's two unused divisions (XII Corps) under Williams and Geary (the latter a future governor of Pennsylvania). The position had lost more than two-thirds of its strength late that afternoon when Meade ordered Williams's division, then Geary's, to move south to help beat off *Longstreet's* attacks. Only Brigadier General George Greene's small brigade was left behind to defend the long Federal position. Geary was merely told to follow Williams's division, but he got lost in the darkness and led his unit two miles southeast of Baltimore Pike, well off the battlefield.

The troops had spent much of the day scraping up enough loose dirt and rocks to make a low breastwork. They placed logs and fence rails between the boulders to make the position stronger. Occupying a position to the right of Wadsworth's division, Greene's brigade now had no troops to its right to defend the mile-long hill that had been held by 10,000 men only a short time before. Sixty-three-year old "Pop" Greene, the oldest man in either army, knew better than to spread his men too thin, but he did extend them partway to the right, then pulled his flank back at a right angle so it faced south while the rest of his line faced east.

When *Johnson's* division finally attacked in the gathering gloom, Greene offered encouragement to his men, walking back and forth along the line. It was a classic engagement involving a hopelessly outnumbered unit attempting to hold its position. Wadsworth sent units to bolster Greene, as did Hancock and Howard, but the line was still terribly thin. After at least four Rebel charges, *Steuart's* brigade finally drove the defenders out of some of their trenches at 9:30.

Soldiers have never particularly liked night fighting. Targets are hard to see and everything looks different in the darkness, even for those with little imagination. As though by common consent, the firing ceased. Both sides seemed content to wait for daylight to renew the hostilities. It was a most unfortunate decision for the Confederates. Without knowing it, *Johnson's* division was within 200 yards of Baltimore Pike, Meade's lifeline to Baltimore and Washington, and squarely on the Union army's right flank and rear. It was an opportunity that seldom occurs on a battlefield and should have been exploited immediately.

The XII Corps was ordered back to its original positions on Culp's Hill later that night, after Meade was satisfied that conditions had stabilized on Cemetery Ridge. One can probably understand the feelings of the officers and men, tired and hungry from their long hike, when they found their trenches filled with Confederates. The two divisions had no choice but to bivouac in the fields along Baltimore Pike and wait until the first light of July 3.

DAY TWO ENDS

It had been a nerve-wracking day at Union army headquarters, with one crisis after another, any one of which could have brought disaster to the hard-luck Army of the Potomac and sent George Gordon Meade into the growing ranks of its repudiated former commanders. Meade's personal evaluation of the results of the battles of July 1-2 have not been recorded and he could not have known at the time just how extensively the Confederate leaders had blundered. He did know that Union forces had narrowly escaped disaster on both days, but at least had inflicted comparable losses on the enemy. His army's morale was high after repulsing the Confederate thrusts on July 2. Although conducting a passive defense, their new commanding general had managed his part with great skill, a rare trait in past army commanders. Equally important, the army occupied an extremely good defensive position. As newly appointed I Corps commander, Brigadier General John Newton told Meade that night, "They have hammered us into a solid position they cannot whip us out of."

Despite massive attacks on all parts of the Union position, *Lee* had only *Johnson's* partial possession of Culp's Hill to show for a day of hard fighting. Again, he was plagued by poor coordination and leadership from his generals. Much of the blame was his for not supervising his two new corps com-

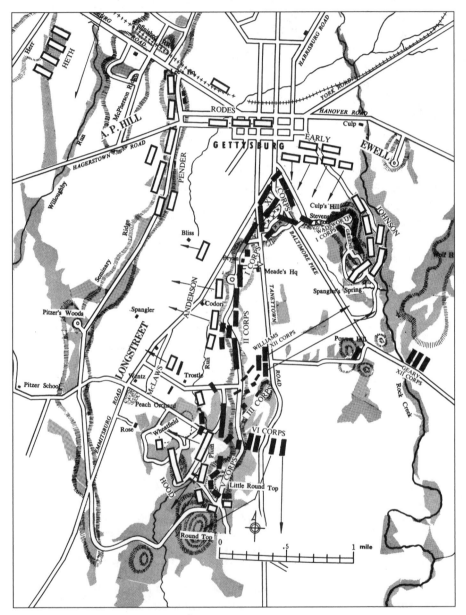

Map 7. Ewell's attack and the situation at dark, July 2.

manders. In this regard, Meade fared much better. He had taken a much more active role, and his men had fought exceptionally well against a determined foe. As *Lee* had predicted, all of his blunders were exploited by Meade, particularly the uncoordinated attacks that permitted Meade to effectively shift troops to blunt *Lee's* efforts without hindrance. *Longstreet's* corps had fought exceptionally well, *Ewell's* less so, and with the exception of part of *Anderson's* division, *Hill's* corps had been hardly engaged.

THE THIRD DAY, JULY 3

MEADE'S COUNCIL OF WAR

When quiet finally settled over the battlefield, George Meade summoned his corps commanders to his headquarters at the Leister House to review the day's events and discuss plans for the next day. Crammed into a ten-by-twelve foot room were Meade, two staff officers, and nine commanding generals. The only non-West Pointer, III Corps commander Daniel Sickles, wasn't there because surgeons had amputated his wounded leg that evening. These highly trained, professional soldiers discussed the situation while sitting on chairs, the bed, or leaning against the walls. General Warren was so exhausted that he slept in a corner.

The group first discussed the day's events and the army's heavy losses. There was concern about dwindling supplies—the wagon train was more than twenty miles away. Finally, the discussion focused on the future. Meade's chief of staff, Major General Daniel Butterfield, asked the group to discuss and informally vote on three questions: Should the army remain where it was or move closer to its base of operations? If the decision was to stay, should the army attack or remain on the defensive? If the latter, how long should the army wait for an attack? Though there were varying opinions, all agreed that the army should remain and fight on the defensive. Being familiar with *Lee's* aggressiveness, most were sure that they would be attacked again the next day. Upon leaving the meeting, Meade prophetically told Gibbon, who commanded the division in the center of the Union line on Cemetery Ridge, "If *Lee* attacks tomorrow, it will be on your front."

LEE STILL CONFIDENT OF VICTORY

Robert E. Lee was also active that night, but he harbored no thoughts of leaving the field. Although his army had not achieved its objective of driving the Federals off the hills, his men had fought splendidly and were close to victory. Despite his disappointment over the results of the second day, he kept these feelings to himself and remained optimistic.

Lee reasoned that the Federal army's near disaster during the first two days of the battle had hurt its morale, while his own men's had increased. His army was now fully assembled except for two small cavalry brigades guarding the mountain passes along his return route to Virginia. *Pickett's* division of *Longstreet's* corps had arrived that afternoon, as had *Stuart's* three cavalry brigades, somewhat the worse for wear but still capable of playing a role.

Lee's optimism was not well-founded. Though Meade may have sustained higher losses up to this point, they were compensated for by the overall larger size of the Union army, which was now completely on the field and had 20,000 more men than the Confederates. Even though the I, III, and XI corps had almost been destroyed, and the II and V Corps had suffered heavy losses, Meade had two relatively fresh corps (VI and XII). These five divisions contained more than 25,000 fresh soldiers. As important, the morale of the Federals, rather than being in a low state, was excellent. For the first time, the Army of the Potomac had not only stood its ground but had repelled every enemy assault. The Union army, from top to bottom, had developed confidence in its strength and position and was ready to meet *Lee's* next move with vigor.

About the same time that Meade was convening his council of war, *Lee* was welcoming back a wayward guest. His cavalry commander, *J.E.B. Stuart*, had finally returned to headquarters. *Lee* was a gracious man. Never given to intended insult, he masked his feelings well. But on this night he had trouble containing them. As *Stuart* stood before him, he raised his arm in a questioning gesture and merely said, *"General Stuart*, where have you been? I have not heard a word from you for days, and you are the eyes and ears of my army." According to one witness, *Stuart* "wilted" as he explained his actions, including the capture of 150 wagons, which in the long run only slowed his progress. *Lee* responded that he needed his help and that they would not discuss his absence further. This was perhaps the strongest censure ever delivered by *Lee*, for he did not need to deliver strong words for their meaning to be powerful.

Lee's original plan for July 3 is unclear. It appears that *Longstreet* was to continue attacking the Federal left while *Ewell* would assail Meade's right on Culp's Hill. *Stuart's* cavalry would swing around Gettysburg to the east of *Ewell's* corps to take the Union line in reverse and prepare to turn the expected Confederate breakthrough into a Union rout. If this had been the plan, it was changed during the morning of July 3.

THE FIGHT FOR CULP'S HILL
4:30 A.M., JULY 3

Lee's timetable prescribed that the battle open "in the early gray of the morning," but for a third day, his plans went awry. During the night, *Ewell* sent two brigades from *Rodes's* division and one from *Early's* to support *Johnson's* renewed attack on Culp's Hill. Meade repositioned his more numerous artillery that already was on the hill and brought up additional guns for the attack he knew would come.

At about 4:30 A.M., Meade's artillery opened the action by shelling *Johnson's* position. Because of inferior positions and the dense woods, *Johnson's* artillery could not effectively counter the fire. The Federal bombardment had a lethal effect on *Johnson's* infantry, which was ordered up the hill to escape the deluge. The men almost immediately collided with Geary's division, which, with the rest of Slocum's XII Corps, was eager to regain the trenches on the eastern slope that the Confederates had captured the evening before.

The third day's battle thus got under way, initiating an orgy of killing on Culp's Hill that matched the contests on the second day. So terrific was the artillery and musket fire that the forest's foliage was swept away as though a hurricane had passed through the area. Some trees had close to 200 bullets imbedded in their trunks and, for a half century after the battle, this "plateau of death" remained desolate.

Geary's men waited until the Southerners were within 100 yards, then opened fire, and the attackers were swept away by a hail of iron. The carnage was horrendous. Several times, Confederate units swept up the heavily wooded hill; each time, they were thrown back with devastating losses.

The intense fighting continued, hour after hour. When the Confederates were not charging up the hill, the two sides were exchanging sniper fire. At one point, two of *Johnson's* brigade commanders protested new orders to attack the hill, declaring that it was suicidal. *Johnson* was not to be deterred. The men gamely rushed up the hill, only to be slaughtered, their bodies falling among the growing piles of Southern dead and wounded. The Federal infantry were skillfully moved around to ensure that it was fresh, had good fields of fire, and that the storm of lead never relented. Counterattacking, two Federal brigades finally pushed *Steuart's* men out of their captured fortifications.

The Confederate commanders were not the only ones sacrificing lives. After several hours of fighting, Slocum thought the Confederates were withdrawing, so the 2d Massachusetts and 27th Indiana of Ruger's brigade (Williams's division) were ordered to charge across an open field. Upon hearing the order, an incredulous Colonel Charles Mudge of the 2d Massachusetts asked an aide if he was certain of its veracity. Yes, the man said. Mudge replied "It's murder, but it is the order," and led his men forward. Waiting behind a stone wall were two brigades of Southerners who blew the regiments apart as they reached the center of the field. Somehow, the 2d Massachusetts reached the wall before being forced to retreat. Among the dead was Mudge.

For seven long hours, until 11:00 A.M., the battle continued. In the end, having lost ground and sustaining terrible losses, the Confederates gave up the field. *Johnson* lost 30 percent of his division. The 3d North Carolina entered the day with 300 men and ended with 77, a loss of almost 75 percent. One of the men who died was Wesley Culp of the 2d Virginia, who fell at a place overlooking the house where he was born. Because of their defensive stance and the protection of their fortifications, the Federals lost only 8 percent of the XII Corps. The Union had won the first round of the third day's battle—its right flank had passed a grisly test.

LEE PLANS GRAND FINALE

Contrary to his custom, *Longstreet* did not visit *Lee's* command post after the second day's battle. Perhaps their intimate relationship was strained by their disagreement over the plan of battle. They finally met early on July 3 when *Lee* rode over to see *Longstreet*. The sounds of *Johnson's* attacks were reverberating across the fields, but *Longstreet* had not resumed his attack. *Lee* now realized that he and *Longstreet* had miscommunicated once again. Rather than continuing the action broken off the night before, *Longstreet* was ordering a flanking movement against the Union right.

Knowing *Longstreet's* move would not succeed, *Lee* scrapped his plans and cast about for a new approach. Surveying the Union center, he must have liked what he saw. The troops there were exposed, and a concentrated artillery barrage could probably cause serious damage. Also, the open fields in front of the Cemetery Ridge would allow his attacking formations free movement. If his troops were successful, they could assault Slocum's XII Corps from the rear. Thinking back to the day before, he may have remembered how close *Wright's* brigade came to capturing Cemetery Ridge. Perhaps with adequate support, he would have been successful. Now, not just one brigade would be thrown against the distinctive clump of trees on the ridge, but eleven would aim for it.

Longstreet did not like *Lee's* new plan any better than the previous one, and he bluntly repeated that a maneuver around Meade's left flank was far more likely to succeed than a frontal assault. His men would be forced to traverse open fields over hundreds of yards under heavy cannon and small-arms fire. Such an attack was suicidal, he reasoned. *Lee*, unmoved by *Longstreet's* entreaties, merely replied, "The enemy is there, *General Longstreet*, and I am going to strike him." "Old Pete" finally stated that what was being asked of his troops, victorious on so many fields, just could not be done. With growing impatience, *Lee* informed him that he had made up his mind.

In the initial plan, *Longstreet* was to use all three of his divisions in the attack. He was able to convince *Lee*, however, that pulling *Hood* and *McLaws* away from the front and moving them to the left would suggest a pullout and invite an attack. *Lee* agreed to leave them in their positions. He substituted two of *Hill's* divisions, but *Longstreet* would still command the four-division attack.

Pickett's newly arrived division would form the center of the attacking line. *Wilcox's* and *Perry's* brigades (*Anderson's* division) would form on *Pickett's* right and move forward over approximately the same ground they had traversed the day before, when they had almost captured Cemetery Ridge. *Heth's* division, now commanded by *Pettigrew*, would form on *Pickett's* left. Two brigades of *Pender's* division, now commanded by *Isaac Trimble*, would form behind *Pettigrew*. The old warrior, who had been unable to persuade *Ewell* to attack Culp's Hill on the first day of battle, could now attack his own heights.

The choice of units was curious. Of *Anderson's* five brigades, the two that had suffered the lightest losses the day before (*Mahone's* and *Posey's*) were not used. On the other flank were brigades like *Archer's* and *Davis's* of *Heth's* division, which had been mauled on the first day's battle. In *Pender's* division, instead of using the relatively fresh brigade under *Thomas*, *Lee* included *Scales's* devastated brigade. This unit had already lost its commander, and every field officer but one was dead or wounded. These were certainly not units to be used in such an attack.

The brunt was directed against Hancock's II Corps. While it had assisted in repelling flank attacks the day before, the corps was comparatively fresh. The target of the assault, the copse of trees, was held by Brigadier General Alexander Webb's Philadelphia Brigade (Gibbon's division), which had helped to beat back *Wright's* brigade the day before. At most, there were 5,750 infantry and twenty-three guns to contest the charge in this sector. Nevertheless, about 100 Federal guns from Cemetery Hill down to Little Round Top could pour fire on the fields that *Longstreet's* men would cross. Sixty others were in reserve.

Colonel E. Porter Alexander was in charge of the Confederate artillery barrage. When the Federal guns were silenced and the supporting infantry dazed, *Alexander* was to order the infantry to advance. Merely a colonel, he did not want the responsibility of launching the attack, so he tried to put it back on *Longstreet*, where it rightfully belonged. Finally, it was agreed that *Alexander* would merely tell *Pickett* when he thought the attack should be launched. Given the distances and the smoke that would shroud the field, the decision could only be based on a weakening of the Union artillery's response.

Before long, battery after battery was wheeled into position until about 140 guns bristled along the Confederate line from the Peach Orchard north to Oak Hill, about two miles. Ammunition was scarce, so *Alexander* ordered the gunners to not fire until ordered. And because preparations took longer than expected, the attack did not commence at 10:00 A.M. as planned. *Hill's* gunners ignored *Alexander's* orders at about 11:00 A.M., and sixty-three cannon opened up on skirmishers around the Bliss barn. They fired for nearly thirty minutes but did little to the Union forces.

As the temperatures climbed toward 87 degrees with high humidity, the infantry designated for the frontal assault moved onto the reverse slope of Seminary Ridge, out of sight of the Federals. Hours passed.

On the opposite ridge, a group of Union generals, including Meade, Hancock, Gibbon, Newton, and Cavalry Commander Alfred Pleasonton, sat on cracker boxes and a fallen log. They had just concluded a meager lunch and were having a smoke before returning to their troops. It was 1:07 P.M.

Suddenly, the world seemed to explode. In response to two signal guns at the Peach Orchard, all 140 Confederate field pieces opened with solid shot and shell. Hunt's artillery responded. The roar of more than 200 guns ushered in the most stupendous artillery duel ever fought on American soil. The battlefield was soon covered with smoke and dust, through which little could be seen except muzzle flashes and the exploding shells that tore into men and horses on both ridges. One Northerner later wrote, "The air was full of grass and dirt cast from the soil by the jagged rebel iron. . .There seemed to be no place where they did not strike and no spot from whence they did not come."

When the bombardment opened, Hancock's infantrymen grabbed their guns and rushed forward to their positions behind stone walls and rail fences about 100 yards below the crest of the ridge. As a consequence, the Union infantry lying on the forward slope of the ridge suffered little damage because the Confederate gunners were firing too high. The Philadelphia Brigade lost only about fifty men during the cannonade. The real victims of this fire were the Union artillery reserve, supply and ammunition dumps, and medical personnel. Every living thing that chanced to be in the impact area took a beating that troops seldom have to endure.

Many of *Pickett's* units were exposed to return fire and took several direct hits. As many as 300 were killed or wounded while waiting to make the charge. One regiment lost almost ninety men.

Meade's headquarters, located several hundred yards behind the clump of trees on the crest of Cemetery Ridge, was at the center of the impact area. Miraculously, none of Meade's staff officers was hit, but sixteen horses were killed. It was no place to transact army business, so the whole outfit moved over to Slocum's headquarters on Power's Hill, beyond the range of the guns on Seminary Ridge.

Many of the men were surprised to discover General Hancock riding along his lines with the II Corps flag unfurled behind him. Although risky, his bravado achieved its intended result—the men felt calmer and reassured that their commander was not frazzled by the situation. One of his brigade commanders said, "General, the corps commander ought not to risk his life that way." Hancock smiled and replied, "There are times when a corps commander's life does not count."

Alexander had thought that the cannonade would last ten to fifteen minutes, but the return fire was so intense that he continued the bombardment for more than an hour and a half. Hunt handled his guns superbly, quickly replacing batteries that were destroyed or had exhausted their ammunition. Foreseeing the infantry assault, Hunt decided to conserve his ammunition so that each gun would have enough left to sweep the Confederates off the fields.

Sensing that the Federal fire was slackening, *Alexander* sent a message to *Pickett*: "For God's sake come quick. . .unless you advance quick my ammunition won't let me support you properly." *Alexander* had actually fallen for a ruse. When he thought the time was right, Hunt reduced the firing and pulled several guns from the line, giving the impression that they were retreating. He was merely replacing several damaged batteries so that the Southern infantry would charge against a ridge still bristling with Union cannon.

THE *PICKETT-PETTIGREW-TRIMBLE* CHARGE
3:00 P.M., JULY 3

When *Pickett* got *Alexander's* message, he rode over to *Longstreet*, saluted, and showed it to him. "General, shall I advance?" he asked. Overcome by emotion about an attack that he knew would fail, *Longstreet* could not speak. He merely nodded. *Pickett* wheeled, rode to the center of the long line, and gave a short speech: "Up, men, and to your posts! Don't forget today that you are from Old Virginia. . . .Forward, guide center, march!"

As the gray lines moved out from the sheltering woods on Seminary Ridge at 3:00 P.M., as if on dress parade, a dramatic silence settled over the battlefield. It was as though the curtain had risen on the last act and the orchestra was waiting for the cue to resume. Down the slight grade toward Emmitsburg Road they marched, forty-one fluttering regimental battle flags adding color to the impressive scene. Bands played "Dixie" as the men left the ridge and the cannoneers cheered.

Pickett's division moved forward in two waves (See Map 8, p. 103). Each consisted of two ranks followed by a line of file closers. On the right was *Brigadier General James Kemper's* brigade; to his left was *Brigadier General Richard Garnett's*. Following *Garnett* by about 100 yards was *Pickett's* third brigade under *Brigadier General Lewis Armistead*. A glance to his left showed *Pickett* that *Pettigrew's* and *Trimble's* divisions had also begun their advance. There was no sign of movement to *Pickett's* right, where *Wilcox's* and *Perry's* brigades were to jump off.

It was now time for *Alexander* to move up some guns he had carefully put aside to support the advance. To his horror, he learned that *Lee's* chief of artillery, *Brigadier General William Pendleton*, had moved them to other parts of the battlefield. Worse, the ammunition for his remaining guns was low, and because the supply trains were so far in the rear, many of the guns would remain silent when they were needed most. Inadequate artillery support helped doom the charge. *Longstreet* was stunned when he heard the report and angrily ordered his aides to stop the charge. It was too late.

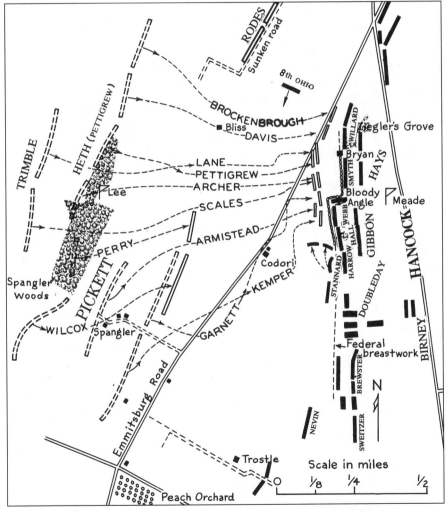

Map 8. The Pickett-Pettigrew-Trimble assault (known as Pickett's Charge), July 3.

Since Union guns on Cemetery Ridge also were running low on long-range shells, they remained silent until *Pickett's* men neared Emmitsburg Road. The guns on Cemetery Hill apparently had an adequate supply and opened sooner on *Pettigrew's* men. As the units reached the road, their formations were broken by the sturdy fences that ran on both sides of it. Upon climbing the fences, the men were exposed to a raking artillery fire. One observer later wrote that the Confederates "were at once enveloped in a dense cloud of dust. Arms, heads, blankets, guns, and knapsacks were tossed into the clear air. A moan went up from the field distinctly to be heard among the storm of battle."

The Federal artillery fire had a devastating effect on the packed Confederate lines. As many as ten men went down in one shell burst. As veterans, they merely closed ranks and continued, elbow to elbow. Virtually every shell hit its mark. No man could long live in such a maelstrom of death—only by reaching Cemetery Ridge could the men be spared. The Union soldiers watched the Southerners advance in awe. Veterans of many battles, they had never seen such a spectacle.

Because of the terrain and the fact that they were aiming for the ground around the copse of trees, a gap of about 1,000 feet separated *Pickett's* and *Pettigrew's* men. As the lines moved forward, the gap narrowed, but still, *Pickett's* men were ordered to make a forty-five-degree turn to the left before again heading toward Cemetery Ridge. In front of the ridge, the ground dipped, allowing officers to correct their alignment without being exposed to fire.

The Union gunners changed from shell to shrapnel, then to canister, and finally, at point-blank range, to double loads of canister. These dreaded antipersonnel charges consisted of twenty-five one-inch iron balls in tin cylinders. Used at short ranges, they have the same effect as a giant shotgun.

The storm of lead caused serious losses among the Confederates, resulting in vast confusion as the initial cohesion evaporated. The thinned ranks advanced with matchless bravery, possibly on the premise that the sooner they reached the Union defenses and faced mostly rifle fire, the greater would be their chances of escaping the artillery. Fortunately for the Confederates on the right flank, the Union guns on Little Round Top—which rarely missed their mark—were masked as *Pickett's* men neared Cemetery Ridge. Otherwise, even fewer would have reached their objective.

THE 8TH OHIO GAINS DISTINCTION

Pettigrew formed the four brigades of his division abreast, each in a double line, on *Pickett's* left flank. The leftmost was *Brockenbrough's* small unit. It had not advanced very far before it was hit by a terrific fire from the thirty-one cannon on Cemetery Hill. Upon reaching a protective swale, the men were ordered to halt and adjust their lines. As they advanced, they passed *Rodes's* division and two brigades from *Pender's* resting along a sunken road on their left. *Brockenbrough's* troops were soon hit by volleys of musketry erupting from their left flank. The day before, the 8th Ohio had been sent forward to support the skirmishers beyond Emmitsburg Road, but it had not been pulled back. As the advance began, the Ohioans watched with interest as the long gray line moved toward Cemetery Ridge. Despite the odds, their commander hit *Brockenbrough's* left flank. After being devastated by massed artillery fire and now under flank attack, the Virginians decided that they had had enough for the day and pulled back to Seminary Ridge.

During this attack, the men of *Rodes's* and *Pender's* divisions, lying nearby in the sunken road, were in a perfect position to both cover the left of *Pettigrew's* attacking line and to advance and neutralize the 8th Ohio. Without orders, the men of these five brigades did nothing—they merely watched the slaughter of their comrades. Once again, an almost complete lack of coordination robbed *Lee* of victory.

With *Brockenbrough's* men fleeing to the rear, the Ohioans turned their attention on the next brigade in line, *Davis's*. They were joined by the 126th New York, and their withering fire broke the Mississippians as well, forcing many to the rear. Taking heavy losses themselves, the men of these two regiments kept up their fire as *Pettigrew's* remaining brigades charged toward Cemetery Ridge.

PICKETT'S RIGHT FLANK DISSOLVES

While *Pettigrew's* leftmost brigades were being decimated by cannon fire from Cemetery Hill, the same was happening to *Pickett's* rightmost brigade under *Kemper*. Many men had fallen from the shells fired from Little Round Top and southern Cemetery Ridge. Seeing *Kemper's* men advancing to his right, Brigadier General George Stannard (Doubleday's division, I Corps) ordered his Vermonters to advance. They were well-trained but had not seen action before Gettysburg. Given their calm demeanor, no one would have known it. Moving forward several hundred yards, they wheeled to the right and fired a crashing volley into *Kemper's* flank. So effective was this fire that the Southern line seemed to evaporate, though some of *Kemper's* left most units edged away, still aiming for the clump of trees. Both ends of the Confederate line had thus fallen victim to artillery fire, then infantry attacks.

Where were *Wilcox's* and *Perry's* brigades, which were to have protected *Kemper's* right flank? Apparently, no one told them to advance with *Pickett's* men and when they finally moved, it was about twenty minutes after the main attack. Making matters worse, they drifted toward the right, leaving a large gap between them and *Kemper*. Their movement therefore was isolated and lost all connection with the main effort. Stannard turned to meet these fresh opponents, blasting their left flank. Bewildered, the two Confederate brigades abandoned their advance and filtered back to their own lines. If they had attacked with *Pickett*, Stannard might have been caught in the middle and destroyed.

The great Confederate charge was coming apart at the seams (actually the flanks), but it might still succeed, if only enough of the 13,000 men who had started out thirty minutes before could remain alive to finish the job.

THE CLIMAX

Having crossed Emittsburg Road, *Pickett's* and *Pettigrew's* survivors approached the stone wall at the base of Cemetery Ridge. Behind the low stone wall lay Federal infantry of Hancock's II Corps, who had been ordered to hold their fire. Behind the stone wall running north and south in front of the copse of trees were the men of General Gibbon's division. About 100 yards to the north (right) of the clump of trees, the wall made a 90-degree turn to the right, and this part of the fence was called the "Angle." The stone fence ran up the ridge for almost another 100 yards before again making another 90-degree turn to the north. To the right of this "Angle," General Alexander Hays posted his men.

On the crest, Hancock's men waited grimly for the order to fire. Closer and closer came the Confederates—200 . . . 150 . . . 100 yards from the stone wall. The Union cannon at the Angle were silent—the men who had served the pieces were dead or wounded. Suddenly, the Union line erupted. Sheets of flame spurted from behind the Federal breastworks, where the men were massed three or four deep. The infantry had collected muskets that were lying around from the prior day's fight with *Wright's* brigade, and they used them to pour additional fire into the Confederates without stopping to reload. Pausing just long enough to return the fire and apparently undeterred by the Union volleys, the mass of Confederates still on their feet covered the last few yards in a rush and, spurred on by the wild Rebel yell, poured over the wall.

In the face of the slaughter, it is surprising that a single man reached the Union defenses along the crest. By the time the front line reached the stone wall to engage in hand-to-hand combat, few had survived. But help was on the way from the second line that included *Armistead's*, *Lane's*, and *Perrin's* brigades.

In front of the mass of men and colors was *Armistead*, with his hat held aloft on the point of his sword. A close friend of Hancock in the prewar army, the two were not to meet on this fatal field, as the Federal commander had already been wounded and carried to a field hospital. So had Gibbon, the division commander, who was temporarily in charge of the II Corps. It was Webb's Philadelphia brigade that *Armistead's* men penetrated, and the initial impact was strong enough to drive many of them away from the stone wall, back over the ridge in a temporary rout from which they were quickly rallied.

A short distance beyond the wall, *Armistead*, his battered hat now down to the hilt of his upheld sword, placed his free hand on the barrel of a silent Union gun as though to confirm its capture. At that moment he was hit by several bullets and fell mortally wounded. Earlier, both *Kemper* and *Garnett* had fallen, the latter also mortally wounded. His body was never found.

Help for the Federal troops was at hand. Like the swinging of two doors, regiments from the left and right of the beleaguered line converged on the Southerners and slammed against their flanks while Webb battled them from the front. Colonel Norman Hall's brigade came charging up at a dead run. So did Brigadier General William Harrow's. Some units of Sickles's shattered III Corps also rushed up in support. Many couldn't get to the Rebels because there were so many comrades in front of them, so they resorted to arching rocks at the enemy. Half of the men who were with *Armistead* were killed and many more wounded. Most of the rest were captured.

To the north of the Angle, the survivors of *Pettigrew's* and *Trimble's* divisions had pushed resolutely ahead. Assailed by sheets of artillery and musket fire from front and flank, they suffered frightful casualties in the comparatively small area north of the Angle. A handful of stalwart Confederates managed to live long enough to get over the wall and into the Union defenses. The bodies of some of *Brigadier General James Lane's* men were found after the battle in the orchard south of Ziegler's Grove. No troops had gotten farther than these gallant men.

Soon the remnants of the once-magnificent array of 13,000 men could be seen dragging themselves back across the valley to the security of Seminary Ridge, leaving the fields dotted with thousands of their dead and wounded. The grand assault took but an hour, but Confederate losses exceeded 50 percent. Some regiments lost as many as 85 percent of their men. The 14th Tennessee (*Archer's* brigade) entered the battle with 365 men. Sixty remained at the conclusion of the first day and only three reported for duty after the charge on the third day. The North's loss was light by comparison, 25 percent.

Lee rode out from Spangler's Woods on Seminary Ridge to meet his returning men, expressing sympathy and concern for them and urging them to rally to repel a counterattack that would surely come. "This was all my fault, *General Pickett*," he said to the brokenhearted leader of the assault. "Your men did all men could do. The fault is entirely my own." To *Wilcox*, *Lee* said, "It is I that have lost this fight, and you must help me out of it the best way you can." When told to reform his division to prepare for a counterattack, *Pickett* merely bowed his head and said, "*General Lee*, I have no division now." He would go to his grave with a strong bitterness toward *Lee* for destroying his fine division.

Over on Cemetery Ridge, the scene was quite different. As the broken gray lines filtered back to their own positions, the men in blue realized the significance of the moment. From Cemetery Hill to Round Top, every man who could do so gazed in sheer disbelief that they had broken the magnificent Confederate charge. Cheer after cheer resounded from the heights. It was the first time that *Lee's* army had been so badly defeated. It could not have come at a better time for the Federal forces. The Army of the Potomac had waited a long time for this moment, and at last it had showed what it could do under intelligent leadership.

Both *Longstreet* and *Lee* expected a counterattack. Meade considered it, but seeing the destruction wreaked on troops crossing the open fields, decided to tend to his dead and wounded and watch for *Lee's* next move.

CAVALRY ACTIONS

Stuart had also been active during the morning. In accordance with *Lee's* orders, he moved his cavalry around *Ewell's* left and, by 2:30 P.M., occupied an elevated wooded region known as Cress Ridge, just to the northeast of Gettysburg. With a force of more than 6,000, *Stuart* was to get behind the Union line on Cemetery Ridge while the infantry attacked from the opposite side.

Brigadier General David Gregg's cavalry division was in the vicinity and, when he spotted *Stuart's* troops in the open, he knew he was in for a fight. It started when dismounted skirmishers on each side opened fire across the fields between the two ridges. Reinforcements arrived and a general engagement developed. After several hours of indecisive intermediate-range shooting, *Stuart* decided that he had to brush aside these Federal horsemen if he was to be of any help to *Lee's* main effort to the west. Two brigades attacked with sabers flashing. They were met by Union artillery and rifle fire that tore gaps in their line but failed to stop them. Brigadier General George Custer, out in front of his brigade, advanced to meet this threat. Increasing from a trot to a gallop, the opposing sides met head-on with an impact so violent that many of the horses were turned end over end, hurling their riders to the ground. What followed was a fierce melee, with charges and countercharges all over the field. Gregg executed a number of flank attacks that seemed to bewilder the Southern horsemen, who were accustomed to Union cavalry withdrawing in face of their mounted charges. The unexpected and surprising resistance of the Federal horsemen (who in this battle, as at Brandy Station, demonstrated that they had learned how to fight) convinced *Stuart's* squadrons that they couldn't win. *Pickett's* charge had long since been turned back, and the cavalry struggle, which had gone on for nearly three hours, finally ended. *Stuart's* brigades withdrew to Cress Ridge and then returned to *Lee's* army west of Gettysburg, while Gregg's cavalry remained in possession of the field.

Another cavalry action was brewing at the southern end of the battlefield. During the artillery duel preceding the Confederate frontal assault, Brigadier General Judson Kilpatrick's cavalry division skirmished inconclusively with *Law's* infantry near the Round Tops. At 5:00 P.M., long after the attack on Cemetery Ridge had been repulsed and the battle essentially was over, Kilpatrick ordered Brigadier General Elon Farnsworth's brigade to mount a full attack on the Confederate infantry. He later tried to justify this charge by saying that he thought Meade had ordered a general counterattack by the infantry on Cemetery Ridge and that he sought to cooperate from his position on the south flank.

Farnsworth considered the order to be virtually suicidal and said so. Hinting that Farnsworth was a coward, Kilpatrick insisted that his orders be obeyed. Farnsworth was no coward, and he reluctantly ordered his men forward. Twice the brigade attacked, only to be repulsed with severe losses. On the third attempt, Farnsworth led the attack in person, taking his 300 troopers in a hell-for-leather mounted attack reminiscent of the Charge of the Light Brigade during the Crimean War. Over rocks and fences, through woods and underbrush, the galloping Federals rode through the positions of the Confederate infantry, then circled about and rode back, picking up about 100 prisoners but suffering more than sixty casualties themselves, including General Farnsworth, who was killed on the return journey.

The third and last day of the Battle of Gettysburg finally ended.

AFTERMATH

With the repulse of the *Pickett-Pettigrew-Trimble* charge, Meade faced a momentous decision: should he counterattack or remain on the defensive? Before being carried from the field, Hancock urged Meade to counterattack. His cavalry commander, Pleasonton, agreed. Others were not so sure. They had watched *Lee* redeploy his artillery and troops, and they knew that despite their heavy losses, the Rebels were still full of fight. They could not see that *Lee's* men were dug in along the western side of Seminary Ridge, ready to repulse anything that Meade threw at him.

Meade had Sedgwick's VI Corps of 15,000 fresh men to spearhead an offensive, but in the end, he wisely held off. The decision was derided through the years as a cowardly one, yet *Lee* and the entire Confederate army desperately wanted Meade to attack. Such an action was doomed and could have changed the outcome of the battle. At the very least, it could have helped salvage some Southern pride.

Lee Withdraws to the Potomac
July 4 to 13

July 4 was a bad day for *Lee*. Frustrated in his attempts to throw Meade off the hills and ridges south of Gettysburg, he realized that his army could no longer take the offensive. Especially worrisome was the fact that his supplies of ammunition and food were dangerously low. Still, he decided to wait one more day for Meade to attack. Knowing that his invasion of the North was over, no matter what Meade did, *Lee* started his seventeen-mile wagon train south for Virginia. He sent his cavalry thundering southward to defend the mountain passes through which his army would cross and sent a message to troops in Virginia to guard his intended crossing point over the Potomac River. As was the case after just about every large battle, the skies opened and torrential rain fell, making *Lee's* return journey all the more difficult.

On the evening of July 4, *Lee* realized that he would not be attacked and began putting his troops on the road. *Hill's* corps took the lead, followed by *Longstreet's* and then *Ewell's*. The darkness covered the withdrawal, so at dawn on July 5, the Army of the Potomac found itself alone on the field.

Sunday, July 5, was half gone before Meade was convinced that *Lee* was withdrawing. He now sent Gregg's cavalry division in pursuit on Chambersburg Pike and started Sedgwick's VI Corps down Fairfield Road to reengage the Confederates, who had already put many miles between them and the enemy.

Meade followed with the remainder of his army on July 7, marching slowly southward in parallel columns east of the mountains. This infuriated Lincoln and other politicians. Vicksburg, Mississippi, had fallen on July 4 and the time was ripe to end the rebellion.

Reaching the Potomac at Williamsport, Maryland, *Lee* was upset to find that the rain had so swollen the river that crossing was impossible. He had to turn his back to the river and erect strong breastworks to fight off any Federal attacks, which were possible from several directions.

Perhaps because of this strong defensive position, *Lee* again hoped that Meade would attack. But when the river fell and it looked as though Meade would not attack, he ordered his men to cross after dark on July 13. He did not know that an attack was planned for the next day. The Confederate army did not get across the river unscathed, however. Its rear guard under *Henry Heth* was attacked and suffered heavy losses, including the mortal wounding of *Pettigrew*. How ironic that the division that opened the fight at Gettysburg was involved in the final engagement of the campaign.

The campaign was over. The North had lost 23,000 men, the South 28,000. The losses among officers were especially severe. It took months for both armies to replenish their ranks and select new officers.

WHEN THE ARMIES LEFT

Three days of combat had left the Gettysburg area in a terrible state. During the battle, the 170,000 combatants had fired 569 tons of metal (50,000 artillery rounds and 7 million small-arms cartridges), resulting in about 51,000 casualties—10,000 killed, 30,000 wounded, and 10,000 missing or captured. The wounded actually exceeded the population of Adams County, Pennsylvania. More than 3,000 horses and mules also died.

Dead men and horses littered the field, some places in piles. While the men left behind diligently tried to bury the 7,000 battlefield dead (3,000 more died of their wounds), it was too big a job and some were not buried for more than a month. The Union dead were buried first, so many Confederates were left to decompose in the July sun. The sights of swollen bodies were sickening and the smells made walking the fields difficult. Hordes of flies also added to the miserable conditions and the potential for an outbreak of disease was serious.

The soldiers from the two armies were buried differently. The Union dead tended to be buried individually and, if their identities were known, a crude headstone was put up. The Confederates were thrown into long, shallow trenches. No body was buried very deeply, so it was not uncom-

Evergreen Cemetery Gatehouse, where the Union generals gathered during the evening of July 1. Taken on July 5, this photograph shows the results of the battle on Cemetery Hill.

mon to see a hand or head sticking out of the soil, especially after heavy rain. The horses were buried or burned, their bones later used as fertilizer.

The first priority, however, was the living. Almost 21,000 nonambulatory men littered the fields, and a lack of manpower meant some of the wounded were in the fields through July 7. Each Federal corps established its own field hospital and at least 100 volunteer hospitals sprang up to care for the wounded in virtually every church and public building, plus many residences. The local hospitals were closed, one by one, as the wounded went to established facilities along the East Coast. The more seriously wounded were sent to a new hospital outside of town called Camp Letterman. The Confederates tried to take as many of their wounded home as possible, but many of the severely wounded were left behind. More than 100 Confederate medical personnel stayed to help care for their 6,000 wounded comrades around Gettysburg. After their work was done, they were infuriated to find that they were considered prisoners of war and were to be sent to internment camps along with the captured soldiers.

For years, no one could doubt that a great battle had been fought around Gettysburg. Few houses and barns escaped damage. Fences were torn down and trees, or what was left of them, were testimony to the ferocity

Modern view of the Gatehouse shows the building's addition. Located on Baltimore Pike, it faces east Cemetery Hill, briefly captured by the Confederates on July 2.

of the battle. Crops were destroyed and many people sued the Federal government for compensation. Although the government agreed with the claims of some, none of the litigants were ever paid.

Scarcely had the two armies departed from Gettysburg when a new one descended upon the area—civilians. Some came to seek out wounded or dead relatives, but most came to satisfy their morbid curiosity. Those arriving within a month of the battle were treated to sights of rotting flesh and amazing quantities of materials of war. Few hesitated to take these items, much to the chagrin of the provost marshal, who quickly published orders that no one was to take any equipment lying around because it belonged to the Federal government. Violators were quickly arrested and for twenty-four to forty-eight hours were put to work burying the dead and assisting in other needed activities. Not even influential individuals were exempt from being pressed into service.

The aftermath included more killing and maiming. For many years after the battle, civilian casualties mounted when individuals tried to disarm "live" artillery shells or were careless with loaded muskets. Plowing the fields around Gettysburg remained a hazardous task for years.

Although the dead of both armies were haphazardly buried after the battle, the Union soldiers were reinterred in the Gettysburg National Cemetery, which was dedicated by Lincoln in November 1863. From 1872 to 1874, Southern women's organizations undertook to reinter Confederate bodies in the South.

The soldiers are all gone now, and the battlefield's scars have disappeared long ago. What remains is the heritage and significance of those three fateful days at Gettysburg.

The number beside the commander of each brigade represents the number of men in the unit; the number in parentheses is the unit's battle losses. The figures are from J. Busey & D. Martin's Regimental Strengths and Losses at Gettysburg, Longstreet House, 1994.

THE ARMY OF THE POTOMAC:

MAJ. GEN. GEORGE MEADE	**93,534**	**(22,813)**

I CORPS: MAJ. GEN. JOHN REYNOLDS

1st Division: Brig. Gen. James Wadsworth	**3,857**	**(2,155)**
1st Brigade: Brig. Gen. Solomon Meredith	1,829	(1,153)
19th IN; 24th MI; 2d, 6th, 7th WI		
2d Brigade: Brig. Gen. Lysander Cutler	2,017	(1,002)
7th IN, 76th, 84th, 95th, 147th NY; 56th PA		
2d Division: Brig. Gen. John Robinson	**2,997**	**(1,690)**
1st Brigade: Brig. Gen. Gabriel Paul	1,537	(1,026)
13th MA; 16th ME; 94th, 104th NY: 107th PA		
2d Brigade: Brig. Gen. Henry Baxter	1,452	(649)
12th MA; 83d, 97th NY; 11th, 88th, 90th PA		
3d Division: Maj. Gen. Abner Doubleday	**4,701**	**(2,103)**
1st Brigade: Brig. Gen. Thomas Rowley	1,361	(898)
80th NY; 121st, 142d, 151st PA		
2d Brigade: Col. Roy Stone	1,317	(853)
43d, 149th, 150th PA		
3d Brigade: Brig. Gen. George Stannard	1,950	(351)
12th, 13th, 14th, 15th, 16th VT		
Artillery Brigade: Col. Charles Wainwright	596	(106)
Guns: 28		
2d, 5th ME Batt; 1st NY Batt L; 1st PA Batt B;		
4th US Batt B		

II CORPS: MAJ. GEN. WINFIELD HANCOCK

1st Division: Brig Gen. John Caldwell	**3,320**	**(1,275)**
1st Brigade: Col. Edward Cross	853	(330)
5th NH; 61st NY; 81st, 148th PA		
2d Brigade: Col. Patrick Kelly	532	(198)
28th MA; 63d, 69th, 88th NY; 116th PA		

3d Brigade: Brig. Gen. Samuel Zook	975	(358)
52d, 57th, 66th NY; 140th PA		
4th Brigade: Col. John Brooke	851	(389)
27th CT; 2d DE; 64th NY; 53d, 145th PA		
2d Division: Brig. Gen. John Gibbon	**3,608**	**(1,647)**
1st Brigade: Brig. Gen. William Harrow	1,366	(768)
15th MA; 19th ME; 1st MN; 82d NY		
2d Brigade: Brig Gen. Alexander Webb	1,244	(491)
69th, 71st, 72d, 106th PA		
3d Brigade: Col. Norman Hall	922	(377)
19th, 20th MA; 7th MI; 42d, 59th NY		
3d Division: Brig Gen. Alexander Hays	**3,644**	**(1,291)**
1st Brigade: Col. Samuel Carroll	977	(211)
14th IN; 4th, 8th OH; 7th WV		
2d Brigade: Col. Thomas Smyth	1,069	(360)
14th CT; 1st DE; 12th NJ; 10th, 108th NY		
3d Brigade: Col. George Willard	1,508	(714)
39th, 111th, 125th, 126th NY		
Artillery Brigade: Capt. John Hazard	605	(149)
Guns: 28		
1st NY Lt. Batt; 14th NY Batt; 1st RI Batt A, Batt B;		
1st US Batt I; 4th US Batt A		

III CORPS: MAJ. GEN. DANIEL SICKLES

1st Division: Maj. Gen. David Birney	**5,095**	**(2,011)**
1st Brigade: Brig. Gen. Charles Graham	1,516	(740)
57th, 63d, 68th, 105th, 114th, 141st PA		
2d Brigade: Brig. Gen. Hobart Ward	2,188	(781)
20th IN; 3d, 4th ME; 86th, 124th NY; 99th PA;		
1st, 2d US Sharpshooters		
3d Brigade: Col. Regis de Trobriand	1,387	(490)
17th ME; 3d, 5th MI; 40th NY; 110th PA		
2d Division: Brig. Gen. Andrew Humphreys	**4,924**	**(2,092)**
1st Brigade: Brig. Gen. Joseph Carr	1,718	(790)
1st, 11th, 16th MA; 12th NH; 11th NJ; 26th PA		
2d "Excelsior" Brigade: Col. William Brewster	1,837	(778)
70th, 71st, 72d, 73d, 74th, 120th NY		
3d Brigade: Col. George Burling	1,365	(513)
2d NH; 5th, 6th, 7th, 8th NJ; 115th PA		
Artillery Brigade: Capt. George Randolph	596	(106)
Guns: 30		

2d NJ Batt B; 1st NY Batt D; 1st RI Batt E;
4th US Batt K; 4th NY Batt

V CORPS: MAJ. GEN. GEORGE SYKES

1st Division: Brig. Gen. James Barnes	**3,418**	**(904)**
1st Brigade: Col. William Tilton	655	(125)
18th, 22d MA; 1st MI; 118th PA		
2d Brigade: Col. Jacob Sweitzer1,	422	(427)
9th, 32d MA; 4th MI; 62d PA		
3d Brigade: Col. Strong Vincent	1,336	(352)
20th ME; 16th MI; 44th NY; 83d PA		
2d Division: Brig. Gen. Romeyn Ayres	**4,013**	**(1,029)**
1st Brigade: Col. Hannibal Day	1,553	(382)
3d, 4th, 6th, 12th, 14th US Regulars		
2d Brigade: Col. Sidney Burbank	954	(447)
2d, 7th, 10th, 11th, 17th US Regulars		
3d Brigade: Brig. Gen. Stephen Weed	1,491	(200)
140th, 146th NY; 91st, 155th PA		
3d Division: Brig. Gen. Samuel Crawford	**2,862**	**(210)**
1st Brigade: Col. William McCandless	1,248	(155)
1st, 2d, 6th, 13th PA Reserves		
2d Brigade: Detached duty		
3d Brigade: Col. Joseph Fisher	1,609	(55)
5th, 9th, 10th, 11th, 12th PA Reserves		
Artillery Brigade: Capt. Augustus Martin	432	(43)
Guns: 26		
5th US Batt D, Batt I; 1st OH Batt L; 3d MA Batt;		
1st NY Batt C		

VI CORPS: MAJ. GEN. JOHN SEDGWICK

1st Division: Brig. Gen. Horatio Wright	**4,215**	**(18)**
1st "Jersey" Brigade: Brig. Gen. Alfred Torbert	1,320	(11)
1st, 2d, 3d, 4th, 5th NJ		
2d Brigade: Brig. Gen. Joseph Bartlett	1,325	(5)
5th ME; 121st NY, 9th, 96th PA		
3d Brigade: Brig. Gen. David Russell	1,484	(2)
6th ME; 49th, 119th PA; 5th WI		
2d Division: Brig. Gen. Albion Howe	**3,610**	**(16)**
2d "1st Vermont" Brigade: Col. Lewis Grant	1,830	(1)
2d, 3d, 4th, 5th, 6th VT		
3d Brigade: Brig. Gen. Thomas Neill	1,775	(15)
7th ME; 33d, 43d, 49th, 77th NY; 61st PA		

3d Division: Maj. Gen. John Newton	**4,740**	**(196)**
1st Brigade: Brig. Gen. Alexander Shaler	1,770	(74)
65th, 675h, 122d NY; 23d, 82d PA		
2d Brigade: Col. Henry Eustis	1,595	(69)
7th, 10th, 37th MA; 2d RI		
3d Brigade: Brig. Gen. Frank Wheaton	1,369	(53)
62d NY; 93d, 98th, 139th PA		
Artillery Brigade: Col. Charles Tompkins	937	(12)
Guns: 48		
1st MA Batt A; 1st, 3d NY; 1st RI Batt C, Batt G;		
2d US Batt D, Batt G; 5gh US Batt F		

XI CORPS: MAJ. GEN. OLIVER HOWARD		
1st Division: Brig. Gen. Francis Barlow	**2,477**	**(1,306)**
1st Brigade: Col. Leopold von Gilsa	1,136	(527)
41st, 54th, 68th NY; 153d PA		
2d Brigade: Brig. Gen. Adelbert Ames	1,337	(778)
17th CT; 25th, 75th, 107th OH		
2d Division: Brig. Gen. Adolph von Steinwehr	**2,894**	**(952)**
1st Brigade: Col. Charles Coster	1,217	(597)
134th, 154th NY; 27th, 73d PA		
2d Brigade: Col. Orland Smith	1,639	(348)
33d MA; 136th NY; 55th, 73d OH		
3d Division: Maj. Gen. Carl Schurz	**3,109**	**(1,476)**
1st Brigade: Brig. Gen. Alexander Schimmelfening	1,683	(807)
82d IL; 45th, 157th NY; 61st OH; 74th PA		
2d Brigade: Col. Wladimir Kryzanowski	1,420	(669)
58th, 119th NY; 82d OH; 75th PA; 26th WI		
Artillery Brigade: Maj. Thomas Osborn	604	(69)
Guns: 26		
1st OH Batt I, Batt K; 4th US Batt G; 1st NY Batt I;		
13th NY Batt		

XII CORPS: MAJ. GEN. HENRY SLOCUM		
1st Division: Brig Gen. Alpheus Williams	**5,256**	**(533)**
1st Brigade: Col. Archibald McDougall	1,835	(80)
5th, 20th CT; 3d MD; 123d, 145th NY; 46th PA		
2d Brigade: Brig. Gen. Henry Lockwood	1,818	(174)
1st MD Eastern Shore,		
1st MD Potomac Home Brigade; 150th NY		
3d Brigade: Brig. Gen. Thomas H. Ruger	1,598	(279)
27th IN; 2d MA; 13th NJ; 107th NY; 3d WI		

2d Division: Brig. Gen. John Geary   **3,964**   **(540)**

1st Brigade: Col. Charles Candy   1,798   (139)
5th, 7th, 29th, 66th OH; 28th, 147th PA

2d Brigade: Brig. Gen. Thomas Kane   700   (98)
29th, 109th, 111th PA

3d Brigade: Brig. Gen. George Greene   1,424   (303)
60th, 78th, 102d, 137th, 149th NY

Artillery Brigade: Lt. Edward Muhlenberg   391   (9)
Guns: 20
1st NY Batt M; PA Lt. Batt E; 4th US Batt;
5th US Batt K

CAVALRY CORPS: MAJ. GEN. ALFRED PLEASONTON

1st Division: Brig. Gen. John Buford   **4,073**   **(176)**

1st Brigade: Col. William Gamble   1,600   (99)
8th, 12th IL; 3d IN; 8th NY

2d Brigade: Col. Thomas Devin   1,148   (28)
6th, 9th NY; 17th PA; 3d WV

Reserve Brigade: Brig. Gen. Wesley Merritt   1,321   (49)
6th PA; 1st, 2d, 5th, 6th US

2d Division: Brig. Gen. David Gregg   **2,614**   **(56)**

1st Brigade: Col. John McIntosh   1,311   (35)
1st MA; 1st MD; 1st NJ; 1st, 3d PA

2d Brigade: Detached Duty

3d Brigade: Col. Irwin Gregg   1,263   (21)
1st ME; 10th NY; 4th, 16th PA

3d Division: Brig. Gen. Judson Kilpatrick   **3,902**   **(305)**

1st Brigade: Brig. Gen. Elon Farnsworth   1,925   (98)
5th NY; 18th PA; 1st VT; 1st WV

2d Brigade: Brig. Gen. George Custer   1,934   (257)
1st, 5th, 6th, 7th MI

Horse Artillery

1st Brigade: Capt. James Robertson   493   (8)
Guns: 28
2d US Batt B, Batt L, Batt M; 4th US Batt E;
6th NY Batt; 9th MI Batt

2d Brigade: Capt. John Tidball   276   (15)
Guns: 20
1st US Batt E, Batt G, Batt K; 2d US Batt A

Artillery Reserve: Brig. Gen. Robert Tyler   **2,376**   **(242)**

1st Reg. Brigade: Capt. Dunbar Ransom   445   (68)
Guns: 24

1st US Batt H; 3d US Batt F; 4th US Batt C;
5th US Batt C

1st Vol. Brigade: Lt. Col. Freeman McGilvery	385	(93)
Guns: 22		
5th, 9th MA Batt; 10th, 15th NY Batt; PA Lt. Batt C,		
Batt F		
2d Vol. Brigade: Capt. Elijah Taft	241	(8)
Guns: 12		
2d CT Batt; 5th NY Batt		
3d Vol. Brigade: Capt. James Huntington	431	(37)
Guns: 20		
1st NH Batt; 1st OH Batt H; 1st PA Batt F, Batt G;		
1st WV Batt C		
4th Vol. Brigade: Capt. Robert Fitzhugh	499	(36)
6th ME Batt; MD Batt A; 1st NJ Batt; 1st NY Batt K;		
1st NY Batt G		

THE ARMY OF NORTHERN VIRGINIA:
GEN. ROBERT E. LEE   70,226 (22,874)

I CORPS: LT. GEN. JAMES LONGSTREET		
Maj. Gen. John Bell Hood's Division	**7,375**	**(2,372)**
Brig. Gen. Evander Law's Brigade	1,933	(500)
4th, 15th, 44th, 47th, 48th AL		
Brig. Gen. Jerome Robertson's Brigade	1,734	(603)
3d AR; 1st, 4th, 5th, TX		
Brig. Gen. George Anderson's Brigade	1,874	(722)
7th, 8th, 9th, 11th, 59th GA		
Brig. Gen. Henry Benning's Brigade	1,420	(519)
2d, 15th, 17th, 20th GA		
Maj. Mathis Henry's Artillery Battalion	403	(27)
Latham's, Bachman's, Garden,s and Reilley's Batteries		
Maj. Gen. Lafayette McLaws's Division	**7,153**	**(2,294)**
Brig Gen. Joseph Kershaw's Brigade	2,183	(649)
2d, 3d, 7th, 8th, 15th SC; 3d SC Battery		
Brig. Gen. William Barksdale's Brigade	1,620	(747)
13th, 17th, 18th, 21st MS		
Brig. Gen. Paul Semmes's Brigade	1,334	(432)
10th, 50th, 51st, 53d GA		
Brig. Gen. William Wofford's Brigade	1,627	(370)
16th, 18th, 24th GA; Cobb's Legion; Phillips's Legion		

Col. Henry Cabell's Artillery Battalion	378	(52)
Manly's, Carlton's, Fraser's, McCarthy's Batteries		
Maj. Gen. George Pickett's Division	**5,473**	**(2,904)**
Brig. Gen. James Kemper's Brigade	1,634	(703)
1st, 3d, 11th, 24th VA		
Brig. Gen. Lewis Armistead's Brigade	1,950	(1,223)
9th, 14th, 38th, 53d, 57th VA		
Brig. Gen. Richard Garnett's Brigade	1,459	(948)
8th, 18th, 19th, 28th, 56th VA		
Maj. James Dearing's Artillery Battalion	419	(29)
Guns: 18		
Stribling's, Caskie's, Macon's, Blount's Batteries		
Col. E. Porter Alexander's Battalion	576	(139)
Guns: 24		
Moody's, Gilbert's, Woolfolk's, Jordan's, Parker's,		
Taylor's Batteries		
Maj. Benjamin Eshleman's Battalion	338	(30)
Sqire's, Richardson's, Miller's, Norcom's Batteries		

II CORPS: LT. GEN. RICHARD EWELL

Maj. Gen. Edward Johnson's Division	**6,433**	**(2,002)**
Brig. Gen. George Steuart's Brigade	2,121	(769)
1st MD; 1st 3d NC; 10th, 23d, 37th VA		
Col. Jesse Williams's Brigade	1,104	(389)
1st, 2d, 10th, 14th, 15th LA		
Brig. Gen. James Walker's "Stonewall" Brigade	1,323	(338)
2d, 4th, 5th, 27th, 33d VA		
Brig. Gen. John Jones's Brigade	1,520	(453)
21st, 25th, 42d, 44th, 48h, 50th VA		
Maj. James Latimer's Artillery Battalion	356	(51)
Guns: 16		
Dement's, Carpenter's, Brown's, Raine's Batteries		
Maj. Gen. Jubal Early's Division	**5,460**	**(1,508)**
Brig. Gen. John Gordon's Brigade	1,813	(537)
13th, 26th, 31st, 38th, 60th, 61st GA		
Col. Isaac Avery's Brigade	1,244	(412)
6th, 21st, 57th NC		
Brig. Gen. Harry Hays's Brigade	1,295	(334)
5th, 6th, 7th, 8th, 9th LA		
Brig. Gen. William Smith's Brigade	806	(213)
31st, 49th, 52d VA		

Lt. Col. Hilary Jones's Artillery Battalion	290	(12)
Guns: 16		
Carrington's, Tanner's, Green's, Garber's Batteries		
Maj. Gen. Robert Rodes's Division	**7,873**	**(3,092)**
Brig. Gen. Junius Daniel's Brigade	2,052	(926)
32d, 43d, 45th, 53d NC; 2d NC Bn		
Brig. Gen. Alfred Iverson's Brigade	1,384	(903)
5th, 12th, 20th, 23d NC		
Col. Edward O'Neal's Brigade	1,688	(696)
3d, 5th, 6th, 12th, 26th AL		
Brig. Gen. George Doles's Brigade	1,323	(219)
4th, 12th, 21st, 44th GA		
Brig. Gen. Stephen Ramseur's Brigade	1,027	(275)
2d, 4th, 14th, 30th NC		
Lt. Col. Thomas Carter's Artillery Battalion	385	(77)
Guns: 16		
Reese's, W. Carter's, Page's, Fry's Batteries		
Artillery Reserve		
Dance's Battalion	367	(50)
Guns: 20		
Watson's, Smith's, Cunningham's, Graham's, Griffin's Batteries		
Nelson's Battalion	277	(24)
Guns: 10		
Kirkpatrick's, Milledge's, Massie's Batteries		

III CORPS: LT. GEN. A. P. HILL

Maj. Gen. Henry Heth's Division	**7,458**	**(3,358)**
Brig. Gen. James J. Pettigrew's Brigade	2,581	(1,450)
11th, 26th, 47th, 52d NC		
Brig. Gen. Joseph Davis's Brigade	2,305	(1,030)
2d, 11th, 42d, MS; 55th NC		
Col. John Brockenbrough's Brigade	971	(186)
40th, 47th, 55th VA; 22d VA Bn		
Brig. Gen. James Archer's Brigade	1,197	(684)
1st, 7th, 14th TN; 13th, 5th AL Bn		
Lt. Col. John Garnett's Artillery Battalion	396	(22)
Guns: 15		
Maurin's, Moore's Lewis's, Grandy's Batteries		
Maj. Gen. W. Dorsey Pender's Division	**6,681**	**(2,392)**
Col. Abner Perrin's Brigade	1,882	(593)
1st, 12th, 13th, 14th SC; 1st SC Rifles		

Brig. Gen. James Lane's Brigade   1,734   (792)
   7th, 18th, 28th, 33d, 37th NC
Brig. Gen. Alfred Scales's Brigade   1,351   (704)
   13th, 16th, 22d, 38th NC
Brig. Gen. Edward Thomas's Brigade   1,326   (264)
   14th, 35th, 45th, 49th GA
Maj. William Pogue's Artillery Battalion   377   (34)
   Guns: 16
   Wyatt's, Graham's, Ward's, Brooke's Batteries

Maj. Gen. Richard Anderson's Division   **7,136**   **(2,185)**

Brig. Gen. Cadmus Wilcox's Brigade   1,726   (778)
   8th, 9th, 10th, 11th, 14th AL
Brig. Gen. William Mahone's Brigade   1,542   (110)
   6th, 12th, 16th, 41st, 61st VA
Brig. Gen. Edward Perry's Brigade   742   (455)
   2d, 5th, 8th FL
Brig. Gen. Carnot Posey's Brigade   1,322   (83)
   12th, 16th, 19th, 48th MS
Brig. Gen. Ambrose Wright's Brigade   1,413   (696)
   3d, 22d, 48th GA; 2d GA Battery
Maj. John Lane's Artillery Battalion   384   (36)

Artillery Reserve

McIntosh's Battalion   357   (48)
   Guns: 16
   Rice's, Hurt's, Wallace's, Johnson's Batteries
Pegram's Battalion   375   (51)
   Guns: 20
   Crenshaw's, Marve's, Brander's, Zimmerman's,
   McGraw's Batteries

Cavalry Division: Maj. Gen. J.E.B. Stuart

Brig. Gen. Wade Hampton's Brigade   1,751   (112)
   1st, 2d SC; 1st NC; Cobb's GA Legion; Phillips's
   GA Legion; Jeff Davis MS Legion
Brig. Gen. Fitzhugh Lee's Brigade   1,913   (95)
   1st, 2d, 3d, 4th, 5th VA; 1st MD Bn
Col. John Chambliss's Brigade   1,173   (56)
   2d NC; 9th, 10th, 13th VA
Brig. Gen. Albert Jenkins's Brigade   1,179   (18)
   14th, 16th, 17th VA; 34th, 36th VA Bn
Horse Artillery: Maj. Robert Beckham   434   (4)
   Guns: 15
   Breathed's, W. Griffin's, Hart's, McGregor's Batteries

SUGGESTED READING

Coco, Gregory. *A Strange and Blighted Land—Gettysburg: The Aftermath of a Battle.* Gettysburg, PA: Thomas Publications, 1995.

Coddington, Edwin. *The Gettysburg Campaign—A Study in Command.* Dayton, OH: Morningside Bookshop, 1968.

Frassanito, William. *Gettysburg: A Journey in Time.* New York: Scribner's, 1975.

Gettysburg Magazine. Dayton, Ohio: Morningside Bookshop, published biannually.

Harrison, Kathy G. and John W. Busey. *Nothing But Glory—Pickett's Division at Gettysburg.* Gettysburg, PA: Thomas Publications, 1987.

Hawthorne, Frederick. *Gettysburg: Stories of Men and Monuments as Told by Battlefield Guides.* Gettysburg, PA: Association of Licensed Battlefield Guides, 1988.

Martin, David. *Gettysburg, July 1.* Conshohocken, PA: Combined Books, 1996.

Nye, Wilbur. *Here Come the Rebels!* Dayton, OH: Morningside Bookshop, 1965.

Patterson, Gerard. *Debris of the Battle: The Wounded of Gettysburg.* Mechanicsburg, PA: Stackpole Books, 1997.

Pfanz, Harry. *Gettysburg—The Second Day.* Durham: University of North Carolina Press, 1987.

Pfanz, Harry. *Gettysburg—Culp's Hill and Cemetery Hill.* Durham: University of North Carolina Press, 1993.

Stewart, George. *Pickett's Charge.* Boston: Houghton Mifflin Company, 1959.

Stackpole, Edward. *They Met at Gettysburg.* Mechanicsburg, PA: Stackpole Books, 1956.

Tucker, Glenn. *High Tide at Gettysburg.* Dayton, OH: Morningside Bookshop, 1973.